Healing!
THE CHILDREN'S BREAD

Dr. Enahoro Francis Ovienmhada

Copyright @2021 by Dr. Enahoro Francis Ovienmhada

All rights reserved. No part of this book may be reproduced in any form or by any electronic or mechanical means, including information storage and retrieval systems, without permission in writing from the publisher, except by reviewers, who may quote brief passages in a review.

This publication contains the opinions and ideas of its author. It is intended to provide helpful and informative material on the subjects addressed in the publication. The author and publisher specifically disclaim all responsibility for any liability, loss or risk, personal or otherwise, which is incurred as a consequence, directly or indirectly, of the use and application of any of the contents of this book.

WORKBOOK PRESS LLC
187 E Warm Springs Rd,
Suite B285, Las Vegas, NV 89119, USA

Website: https://workbookpress.com/
Hotline: 1-888-818-4856
Email: admin@workbookpress.com

Ordering Information:
Quantity sales. Special discounts are available on quantity purchases by corporations, associations, and others. For details, contact the publisher at the address above.

ISBN-13: 978-1-953839-89-3 (Paperback Version)
978-1-953839-90-9 (Digital Version)

REV. DATE: 29.01.2021

TABLE OF CONTENTS

Dedication 09

Acknowledgements 10

The Commission 11

The purpose of this book 12

Introduction 14

Liquid Prayers 17

Healing Through Prayer 20

God's Medicine 22

YHVH's Investment 23

God's Medicine Works 24

Taking YHVH's Medicine 26

There Is A Balm In Gilead 29

Healing Covenant 32

God's Medicine And Healing 33

The Breaker Or Violent Anointing 37

Be Healed 1 - 30 44

Suicide 118

My Prayer/Confessions 120

Healing Scriptures 123

Dedication

I dedicate this book to my late father Engr. David Omozokpia Ovienmhada, who first encouraged me to write a Christian book. He once said to me, "I see you have a huge library of Christian books and you are still buying more. You know they are all derived from the bible. With the time you spend reading the bible, you should be able to write books that will bless others too." He did not live to see me write a book. This is the seventh book I have written and the third to be published soon. I offer this book to all, that you may live and not die.

Acknowledgments

I want to specially thank my family - The Ovienmhada Clan, for their love, support and belief in the call of God upon my life: Mrs. Margaret Salami, Daniel Ovienmhada, Mrs. Flora Egbe, Michael Ovienmhada, Davidson Omozokpia, Mrs. Grace Ojougboh, Mrs. Mary Laniyan and Stella Brisibe. Also, my niece Olajumoke Salami. YeHoVaH richly bless and keep you all.

The Commission

"I have called you to be like unto Moses, to call out a people."

"There remaineth therefore, a rest for the people of God." Hebrew 4:9

"Let us therefore fear, lest, a promise being left us of entering into His rest, any of you should seem to come short of it." Hebrew 4:1

"For the earnest expectation of the creature waiteth, for the manifestation of the sons of God." Roman 8:19

"You will never know who you are until you know who God Is"
"The I am that YHVH says I am, that I am"

The purpose of this book

By September 2016, I will be forty years in ministry. In all these years, I have seen many Christians sick, harassed and tormented by the devil.

King David once lamented over the fate of king Saul and in mourning said *"...as though he had not been anointed with oil..."*

Prophet Jeremiah bemoaning the fate of Israel cried out *"...Is there no balm in Gilead..."*?

My observations have led me to the conclusion that about 80% of Church members are sick and a majority of them without help from the pulpit. Many ministers also suffer and die in the same manner as their congregants, like mere men. Some "Christians," in their desperation for help, have gone to witchdoctors and also invoked Eastern gods for their healing.

Because of the confusion regarding healing in the church among the laity and from the pulpit, I decided to write this book, "Healing!!! The Children's Bread" in order to make the case for the availability of healing for God's people, in no uncertain terms. In this writing, I offer you the unquestionable position of God, regarding your health and well-being.

Many today run to pseudo miracle workers, who really are "Church witchdoctors," and there are claims of results but what really happens is that they take away one problem and give you another, an exchange of sickness and disease.

Is there a way out from the curse of sickness and disease? Yes, and YHVH's provided way is the more sure Word of prophesy. Though there are genuinely anointed men of God that can break them off you, YHVH requires all to eat the Word of life and be healed.

I would like to note here that YeHoVaH (YHVH) speaks to His children, and like Mary rightly said *"... Whatsoever He saith unto you, do it..."* John 2:5

"Be Healed 1 - 30" is your month's supply of God's medicine. You can be healed, and all you need do is eat. These Healing Scriptures are for you to memorize; confess them out and use them as prayer points.

YHVH richly bless you as you eat the bread of life. Amen.

Introduction

He that saith, I know him, and keepeth not his commandments, is a liar, and the truth is not in him. 1John 2:4

If we say that we have fellowship with Him, and walk in darkness, we lie, and do not the truth: 1John 1:6

Know ye not, that to whom ye yield yourselves servants to obey, His servants ye are to whom ye obey; whether of sin unto death, or of obedience unto righteousness? Roman 6:16

I am the good shepherd, and know my sheep, and am known of mine. John 10:14.

Does He really know you? Do you really know Him? Do you do His sayings?

In Chapter 8 of my book "There Shall Be A Performance" titled The Key. I was told that love and meekness (obedience) are the keys. Jesus said if you love me, keep my commandments. If our lives are not characterized by love and obedience, then we are vain worshippers. I will dare to say that a majority of "Christians" fall into this category. If the way to life is narrow and only a few find it, then where are the majority? I would like us to read again the above stated scripture and questions, which I am going to repeat for good measure:

I am the good shepherd, and know my sheep, and am known of mine. John 10:14.

Does He really know you? Do you really know Him? Do you do His sayings?

"Christians claim to love God but do not obey Him. They claim to hate the devil but obey him" – Unknown

Then when lust hath conceived, it bringeth forth sin: and sin, when it is finished, bringeth forth death. **Do not err (wander or stray away), my beloved brethren.** James 1:15

When we come to YHVH with love and obedience we can partake at His table the bread of life.

It is very important to realize that we are built upon a sound spiritual foundation and anchored on Jesus the Rock.

We must all come to Jesus, hear His voice and do His sayings.

It is important for us to experience YeHoVaH's investment here and now and not when we die and go to Heaven. Dominion over Satan, sin, sickness and death are ours now.

Many genuinely born again people struggle for lack of knowledge but this book will help you become established using the principle of calling those things which are not as though they were.

My prayer for you is this:

O God that laid the foundation of the earth in the blood of Jesus Christ His Son, I stand on that sure foundation in the name of Jesus Christ and declare: "The I am that YHVH says I am, that I am"; I still the voices of blood speaking against me by the blood of Jesus that speaks of better things. I break forth; I break through into my unlimited destiny. Amen.

Please do not read this book just like any other book, but

read it prayerfully and with intent. The goal is your healing and health. Be Healed in Jesus Name. Amen.

I have used the name of God, YHVH freely in this book. It is part of my little effort in putting God's name back on our lips instead of LORD in many translations.

Dr. Enahoro Francis Ovienmhada

"THE I AM THAT GOD SAYS I AM THAT I AM"

Liquid Prayers

And Moses cried unto the LORD, saying, Heal her (Mariam) now, O God, I beseech thee. Numbers 12:13.

I beseech thee, O LORD, remember now how I have walked before thee in truth and with a perfect heart, and have done that which is good in thy sight. And Hezekiah wept sore. II Kings 20:3

And I wept much because no man was found worthy to open and to read the book, neither to look thereon. Revelation 5:4

Moses cried, Hezekiah shed tears and John wept much. Have you cried unto YHVH?

When we come to God in absolute obedience to His will, the good news is:

"... Weep not: behold, the Lion of the tribe of Judah, the Root of David, hath prevailed ..." Revelation 5:5

Tears are liquid prayers that get the attention of God. How much more will God hear us when our crying becomes a groan?

After seven days Mariam was healed of her leprosy.

Turn again, and tell Hezekiah, the captain of my people, "Thus saith YHVH, the God of David thy father, **I have heard thy prayer, I have seen thy tears:** *behold, I will heal thee: on the third day thou shalt go up unto the house of YHVH." II Kings 20:5*

The last stanza of the old song "On the wings of a dove" declares:

"I cried for my healing both night and day; but faith wasn't forgotten by the Father above; God gave us His sign on the wings of a dove".

Faith has not been done away with. Faith works and like love abides forever.

For by it the elders obtained a good report. Hebrews 11:1-2

In Isaiah chapter 53:1 we have this question ***"Who hath believed our report and to whom is the arm of the Lord revealed"?***

The report is that the price of man's redemption has been paid in full by the Blood of Jesus on the Cross. You are now debt free.

Free from sin, sickness, pain and disease. For whom Jesus the Son of God has made free is free indeed.

Through faith we understand that the worlds were framed by the Word of God, so that things which are seen were not made of things which do appear. Hebrews 11:3

As it is written, I have made thee a father of many nations, before him whom he believed, even God, who quickeneth the dead, and calleth those things which be not as though they were. Romans 4:17

Let us, with words like a paint brush, begin to frame or paint the picture of what ought to be and not what is. The picture of the mountain removed and a beautiful plain in its place. What God says is what IS. What we see, feel, hear and touch is temporary, not what IS.

Many have, with masterful strokes of the tongue, painted instead how big their mountains are. We are not to ask but to command the mountains to move. David spoke to the physical mountain of Gilboa. He painted a picture of what he desired concerning the mountain because his beloved friend Jonathan and king Saul were killed there. ***To this day, there is no rain or dew on that mountain.***

Ye mountains of Gilboa, let there be no dew, neither let there be rain, upon you, nor fields of offerings: for there the shield of the mighty is vilely cast away, the shield of Saul, as though he had not been anointed with oil. 2Samuel 1:21

Let us pray:

Ye mountain of _____ (cancer: T-lymphoma, breast, colon) be plucked up by the roots, wither and die in the redemptive name Jesus (Jehovah saves, heals, delivers). Jesus is glorified in my body. Thank you Lord; for anointing me with the oil of gladness and for the Sun of Righteousness arising with healing in His wings. Amen!!!

Healing Through Prayer

Healing through prayer is God's Medicine. Healing is available to all in God's provisions. Jesus in one place said, "Healing is the children's bread". This reveals that sickness is similar to hunger. Hunger is satisfied by eating the food you desire. Similarly, in sickness you reach out for the cure through healing prayer or healing touch. There is a process that starts with need, desire to meet the need and reaching out for the solution. Sickness is the issue. Prayer is the pathway. Healing is the answer.

The woman with the issue of blood, who had spent her living on doctors, had a need for healing and to stop the drain on her finances. She reached out to YHVH in His covenant. Prayer is believing and standing on the desire in your heart according to the will of God, and making a declaration and acting on it. The covenant of healing was in the Sun of Righteousness' tassels or wings. We are told that the woman with the issue of blood, had heard (to attend to, consider what is or has been said) of Jesus (Yehoshua – YHVH is salvation.)

*When the woman with the issue of blood had **heard of Jesus**, came in the press behind, and touched His garment. For she said, If I may **touch but His clothes**, I shall be healed. And straightway the fountain of her blood was dried up; and **she felt in her body that she was healed of that plague**.* Mark 5:27-29.

Faith comes by hearing God's Word, the testimony of Jesus.

God is the author and provider of all healing. He has provided a pathway for those in need. When we follow that path, we will meet Him in the place of our need. As John G. Lake said, **"If there is a Christian, let him pray. If there is a God, let Him answer"**.

God Is No Respecter Of Any Diseases

Therefore I say unto you, "What things so ever ye desire, when ye pray, believe that ye receive them, and ye shall have them. Mark 11:24.

There is nothing outside of "What things so ever". – This covers AIDS, Cancer, Diabetes, Ebola, bacterial or viral diseases, etc. You might wonder if God had modern diseases in mind. He is Omniscient, and knows the end from the beginning. He declared in the book of Deuteronomy, Chapter 28:61 "*… **Also every sickness, and every plague, which is not written in the book of this law…***"

YHVH knows, He hears and heals every disease. In the book of Acts, we see the believers healed the sick, cast out demons and raised the dead. What a tremendous anointing was available, which was but a down payment. Today, we are faced with very toxic situations and people desperately looking for solutions. However, the "Church" is powerless.

Having a form of godliness, but denying the power thereof: from such turn away. 2Timothy 3:5

To meet the need today, we must have what the early Church had and more. YHVH, gave a down payment of the Spirit to the early Church at Pentecost and promised a full payment for the end of the age.

"The Book of Acts of the Holy Spirit, which was but a down payment, must be fully lived, and then we can demand the full payment".

Heal the sick, cleanse the lepers, raise the dead, cast out devils: freely ye have received, freely give. Matthew 10:8

I am the YHVH that healeth thee. Exodus 15:26

God's Medicine

God has a prescription and a cure for your ailments and all you have to do is take it. No parent would tell the baby or toddler, "Have you taken your medicine?" Parents would administer the meds even up through the age of 10 yrs. From 11 – 18 yrs. they might ask or remind the child to take his/her meds. As an adult, you are on your own. It is however, interesting to note that many believers remain at the babyhood stage of Christianity. Pastors must lay hands on them, anoint them with oil, plead with them to forgive and come to church.

Miracles of healing came in your babyhood stage easily, but now that you ought to be an adult, the miracles are no longer happening. It is because God has more expectation of you to administer His prescriptions.

God's Medicine:

My son, attend to my Words; incline thine ear unto my sayings.

Let them not depart from thine eyes; keep them in the midst of thine heart. **For they are life unto those that find them, and health to all their flesh.** Proverbs 4:20-22

After this manner therefore pray ye: Our Father which art in Heaven, Hallowed be thy name. **Thy Kingdom come. Thy will be done in earth, as it is in Heaven.** Matthew 6:9-10

Beloved, I wish above all things that thou mayest prosper and be in health, even as thy soul prospereth. 3John 1:2

God's will and wish for you is to be healed and live in divine health. The prescription is His Word, so, self-administer the prescription today.

YHVH's Investment

YHVH made an investment on your behalf and it is guaranteed and all you have to do is to make a withdrawal.

To ask today if it is God's will to heal is to deny God. God is not planning to heal you or going to heal you but has already healed you. Knowledge of that truth sets you free and you can shake off the disease and rise from the bed of sickness.

Let's pray right now: YHVH, disease does not glorify you and it is as a result of broken covenant. I repent of my sins and apply the cleansing blood of Jesus and I enter into your oath. *"Satan, the father of disease and its mother sin,* I reject you in the name of Jesus. *I step into the oath and covenant of healing.* Your hold over me is broken and I command sickness and disease to leave now in Jesus name. Amen."

And this is the confidence that we have in Him, that, if we ask any thing according to His will, he heareth us: And if we know that He hears us, whatsoever we ask, we know that we have the petitions that we desired of Him. 1John 5:14-15 *Wherefore lift up the hands which hang down, and the feeble knees; And make straight paths for your feet, lest that which is lame be turned out of the way; but let it rather be healed.*

Hebrews 12:12-13

For it is God which worketh in you, both to will and to do of his good pleasure. Philippians 2:13

He that spared not His own Son, but delivered Him up for us all, how shall He not with Him also freely give us all things? Romans 8:32

Healing and deliverance are YHVH's investment for you. Make a withdrawal today. God's Word is miracle bread, eat it today!!!

God's Medicine Works

A man went to the hospital and was prescribed medication. **Each day he read the label of the medication.** On another visit to the hospital he told the doctor that there has been no change whatsoever in his condition. The doctor asked if he has been taking the drug as prescribed and he said *I read the label three times a day.* The doctor said not to read the labels but take the tablets inside three times a day.

Healing is in the Word and not in the reading of the Word of God. Reading the bible is like reading the label. However, **eating the Word is taking the prescription.**

For they (my Words) are life unto those that find them, and health to all their flesh. Proverb 4:22

For the Word of God is quick (Alive), and powerful, and sharper than any two-edged sword, piercing even to the dividing asunder of soul and spirit, and of the joints and marrow, and is a discerner of the thoughts and intents of the heart. Hebrew 4:12

"The faithful and persistent application of scriptures will bring amazing results and excellence in ministry that generations to come will talk about."

"You have to split (break) the Word to eat the kernel which is spirit and life"

Disease, the foul offspring of its father, Satan, and its mother, Sin, was defiling and destroying the earthly temples of God's children, and there was no deliverer. - John Alexander Dowie

We cannot tolerate or manage Satan, sin, sickness and disease but deal violently with them with the **"Breaker or Violent Anointing".**

How God anointed Jesus of Nazareth with the Holy Ghost and with power: who went about doing good, and *healing all that were oppressed of the devil;* for God was with him. Acts 10:38

He that committeth sin is of the devil; for the devil sinneth from the beginning. For this purpose *the Son of God was manifested, that He might destroy the works of the devil.* 1John 3:8

Jesus Christ the same yesterday, and today, and forever. Hebrews 13:8

Have you eaten your "Miracle Bread" today?

Taking YHVM's Medicine

The sun shines, darkness and shadows are dispelled, pains and diseases creep away, you cannot stumble, righteousness is revealed. Jesus The Sun of Righteousness shines in the regions of the living and the dead with resurrection life. **"Lazarus come forth…; …Thalitha cumi; …Young man, I say unto thee, Arise"**, were the bread (Word) of life administered by Jesus and the dead sprang back to life and were dead no more.

Rise and be healed today as you eat the "Miracle Bread"

And said, ***If thou wilt diligently hearken to the voice of the LORD thy God, and wilt do that which is right in His sight, and wilt give ear to His commandments, and keep all his statutes,*** *I will put none of these diseases upon thee, which I have brought upon the Egyptians: for I am the LORD that healeth thee.* Exodus 15:26

But if the Spirit of Him that raised up Jesus from the dead dwell in you, He that raised up Christ from the dead shall also quicken your mortal bodies by His Spirit that dwelleth in you. Romans 8:11

For the law of the Spirit of life in Christ Jesus hath made me free from the law of sin and death. Romans 8:2

And having spoiled principalities and powers, He made a shew of them openly, triumphing over them in it. Colossians 2:15

It is the spirit that quickeneth; the flesh profiteth nothing: **the Words that I speak unto you, they are spirit, and they are life.** John 6:63

My son, attend to my Words; incline thine ear unto my sayings. Proverbs 4:20

Have you eaten: ***chewed and digested the Word*** of God today? ***The spirit and life cannot be released without meditation.***

God's medicine is God's bread (Word) provided for our healing. God has administered His Word, we publish it and all you have to do is take it. His Word will always prevail.

For they are life unto those that find them, and health to all their flesh. Proverbs 4:22

"Reading the Word is reading labels, eating the Bible is taking God's medicine"

Also every sickness, and every plague, which is not written in the book of this law, them will the LORD bring upon thee, until thou be destroyed. Deuteronomy 28:61.

This is not causative act of God but a permissive act; for God is not the author of sickness and disease, but disobedience will make you vulnerable and bring you under the curse.

Every good gift and every perfect gift is from above, and cometh down from the Father of lights, with whom is no variableness, neither shadow of turning". James 1:17

Christ hath redeemed us from the curse of the law, *being made a curse for us: for it is written, Cursed is every one that hangeth on a tree:* Galatians 3:13

For as the Father raiseth up the dead, and quickeneth them; even so the Son quickeneth whom He will. John 5:21

If the Son therefore shall make you free, ye shall be free indeed. John 8:36

How to take God's Medicine

Meditate (muse, imagine) on Galatians 3:13, speak in tongues over the scripture and when you are fully charged with your imagination and speaking in tongues, you begin to declare:

This sickness, diagnosed or undiagnosed, written or unwritten in the book, is a curse of the law, but I have been redeemed according to Galatians 3:13. I see myself healed, walking and jumping in my imagination. **Hath** is past tense. If I was redeemed; healed by the stripes of Jesus, then, I **am** redeemed, healed by His stripes now. Father, I thank you for my healing and your faithfulness. Amen.

"The faithful and persistent application of scriptures will bring amazing results and excellence in ministry that generations to come will talk about."

There Is A Balm In Gilead

Is there no balm in Gilead; is there no physician there? why then is not the health of the daughter of my people recovered? Jeremiah 8:22

Is there no more healing in the Church; is there no healing bread there? are there no Pastors there? Why are so many sick in the Church? EFOV

Go up into Gilead, and take balm, O virgin, the daughter of Egypt: in vain shalt thou use many medicines; for thou shalt not be cured. To make the wounded whole; Jeremiah 46:11

There is a balm in Gilead

O The cleansing blood,

Cure for the sinning soul

Rest and peace to give.

There is a balm in Gilead,

Yeshua the Son of God.

To heal the broken body.

Wholeness and soundness give.

There is a balm in Gilead,

The Holy Spirit of God.

The Breaker, sets free,

Yokes and burdens gone.

There is a balm in Gilead.

O' yes, yes, yes. Yes, yes, yes, Amen.

There is a balm in Gilead.

"Tears are liquid prayers that flow to the heart of God, and moves the hand of God."

Now therefore, behold, the cry of the children of Israel is come unto me: and I have also seen the oppression wherewith the Egyptians oppress them. Exodus 3:9

And Jesus went forth, and saw a great multitude, and was moved with compassion toward them, and He healed their sick. Matthew 14:14

So Jesus had compassion on them, and touched their eyes: and immediately their eyes received sight, and they followed Him. Matthew 20:34

And when the Lord saw her, **He had compassion on her***, and said unto her, Weep not.* Luke 7:13

And Jesus, moved with compassion, put forth His hand, and touched him, and saith unto him, I will; be thou clean. Mark 1:41

Then Jesus answering said unto them, Go your way, and tell John what things ye have seen and heard; how that **the blind see, the lame walk, the lepers are cleansed, the deaf hear, the dead are raised, to the poor the gospel is preached.** Luke 7:22

Heal the sick, cleanse the lepers, raise the dead, cast out devils: freely ye have received, freely give. Matthew 10:8

The ointment is in His name, the anointing still flows, He is the compassionate Jesus. We have this treasure in earthen vessels, to do the works and show forth His glory today.

"There is a Balm in Gilead.!!! *The Breaker or Violent Anointing is here*. There is a Balm in Gilead, the healing Jesus."

Healing Covenant

YeHoVaH made a covenant of healing and protection with His people when He declared:

"My covenant will I not break, nor alter the thing that is gone out of my lips." Psalms 89:34

Man's part of the covenant was to abide in the secret place of the Most High and under the shadow of the Almighty. Sin and disobedience will keep us out of the covering, and like little chicks become vulnerable to hawks. The covenant – "The Bill of Rights" is the guarantee of every righteous citizen of the covenant and Jesus is the guarantor.

The Believers Bill of Rights (Healing Covenant)

I will say of the LORD, He is my refuge and my fortress: my God; in Him will I trust.

Surely He shall deliver thee from the snare of the fowler, and from the noisome pestilence.

He shall cover thee with His feathers, and under His wings shalt thou trust: His truth shall be thy shield and buckler.

Thou shalt not be afraid for the terror by night; nor for the arrow that flieth by day;

Nor for the pestilence that walketh in darkness; nor for the destruction that wasteth at noonday.

A thousand shall fall at thy side, and ten thousand at thy right hand; but it shall not come nigh thee.

Only with thine eyes shalt thou behold and see the reward of the wicked.

Because thou hast made the LORD, which is my refuge, even the most High, thy habitation;

There shall no evil befall thee, neither shall any plague come nigh thy dwelling.

For He shall give His angels charge over thee, to keep thee in all thy ways.

They shall bear thee up in their hands, lest thou dash thy foot against a stone.

Thou shalt tread upon the lion and adder: the young lion and the dragon shalt thou trample under feet.

Because he hath set his love upon me, therefore will I deliver him: I will set him on high, because he hath known my name.

He shall call upon me, and I will answer him: I will be with him in trouble; I will deliver him, and honour him.

With long life will I satisfy him, and shew him my salvation. Psalms 91:4 -16

My son, forget not my law; but let thine heart keep my commandments: **For length of days, and long life, and peace, shall they add to thee.** Proverbs 3:1-2

Behold, I will bring it health and cure, and I will cure them, and will reveal unto them the abundance of peace and truth. Jeremiah 33:6

YHVH Rapha (I am YHVH that heals you or I am YHVH your Doctor) is God's covenant of healing with you.

Sickness does not glorify God nor does He take pleasure in the death of a sinner.

God wants to do His good pleasure in you. His pleasure is your salvation: healing, wholeness and soundness.

Let us take a hold of the Word of God and be established in the "Bill of Righteousness" our "Healing Covenant".

God's Medicine And Healing

God's medicine and healing brings joy to God's people. God wants all healed because sickness and diseases are the works of God's arch enemy.

Jesus was manifested to destroy the works of the enemy.

"A commitment to obedience to the Word, guarantees YHVH's obligation to perform His Word".

And being fully persuaded that, what He had promised, He was able also to perform. Roman 4:21

Being confident of this very thing, that He which hath begun a good work in you will perform it until the day of Jesus Christ: Philippians 1:6

He that spared not His own Son, but delivered him up for us all, how shall He not with Him also freely give us all things? Romans 8:32

God's Medicine God's

medicine taken as prescribed starts the healing process. Healing is the process, whereby that which is sick, hurt, or maimed is restored back to wholeness and soundness again. The word therapy is derived from the Greek word which means healing. It could be instantaneous, it could be a process. Do not stop the process.

See yourself healed!!!

Then said the LORD unto me, Thou hast well seen: for I will hasten my Word to perform it. Jeremiah 1:12

And said, If thou wilt diligently hearken to the voice of the LORD thy God, and wilt do that which is right in His sight, and wilt give *ear to His commandments, and keep all His statutes, I will put none of these diseases upon thee, which I have brought upon the Egyptians: for **I am the LORD that healeth thee.*** Exodus 15:26

*That he may establish thee today for a people unto himself, and that he may be unto thee a God, as he hath said unto thee, and **as he hath sworn unto thy fathers, to Abraham, to Isaac, and to Jacob.** Neither with you only do I make **this covenant and this oath;** But with him that standeth here with us this day before the LORD our God, and also **with him that is not here with us this day.*** Deuteronomy 29:13-15

That the blessing of Abraham might come on the Gentiles through Jesus Christ; that we might receive the promise of the Spirit through faith. Galatians 3:14

And if ye be Christ's, then are ye Abraham's seed, **and heirs according to the promise.** Galatians 3:29

The Scriptures are God's medicine for your healing. God swore to perform His Word and you can count on His faithfulness and the *"more sure Word of prophecy".*

As you become established in the *"more sure Word of prophecy",* the dawning of a new day of healing and health is certain as the Daystar arises in your heart. Amen.

The Breaker Or Violent Anointing

"Disease, the foul offspring of its father, Satan, and its mother, Sin, was defiling and destroying the earthly temples of God's children, and there was no deliverer. And there I sat with sorrow-bowed head for my afflicted people, until the bitter tears came to relieve my burning heart. Then I prayed for some message, and oh, how I longed to hear some Words from Him who wept and sorrowed for the suffering long ago, the Man of Sorrows and of Sympathies. And the Words of the Holy Ghost inspired in Acts 10: 38 stood before me all radiant with light, revealing Satan as the defiler and Christ as the Healer. My tears were wiped away, my heart was strong, I saw the way of healing, and the door thereto was opened wide, and so I said, "God, help me now to preach that Word to all the dying 'round, and tell them how 'tis Satan still defiles, and Jesus still delivers, for 'He is just the same today."

The Story of John Alexander Dowie; By Gordon P. Gardiner

We cannot tolerate or manage Satan, sin, sickness and disease but deal violently with them with the "Breaker or Violent Anointing."

Passivity was not the marks of the early apostles. They broke territories, Roman territories for the Kingdom of God. The Kingdom of God suffers violence, Jesus said, and the violent take it by force.

Apostles are Sent Ones, sent by the Kingdom of God and are therefore Ambassadors backed by the Kingdom of God and thus empowered by the Breaker, or Violent Anointing.

A deputy was becoming a hindrance to the gospel and Apostle Paul had to make the pronouncement:

And now, behold, the hand of the Lord is upon thee, and thou shalt be blind, not seeing the sun for a season. And immediately there fell on him a mist and a darkness; and he went about seeking some to lead him by the hand. Acts 13:11

Now it happened, as we went to prayer, that a certain slave girl possessed with a spirit of divination met us, who brought her masters much profit by fortune-telling. This girl followed Paul and us, saying, "These men are the servants of the Most High God, who proclaim to us the way of salvation." And this she did for many days. But Paul, greatly annoyed, turned and said to the spirit, **"I command you in the name of Jesus Christ to come out of her."** *And he came out that very hour.* Acts 16:16-18

And God wrought special miracles by the hands of Paul: So that from his body were brought unto the sick handkerchiefs or aprons, and the diseases departed from them, and the evil spirits went out of them. Acts 19:12

Apostle Paul used spiritual weapons from God's armory against his enemies. As a good soldier, you must know your weapons and hear the instructions of your Commanding Officer the Holy Spirit. As covenant men, two things we need – The Holy Spirit upon us and His Words in our mouth (Isaiah 59:21) also, Love and Meekness (Obedience) as our motto.

Holy Ghost, "Breaker Anointing" broke Paul and Silas out of prison.

And suddenly there was a great earthquake, so that the foundations of the prison were shaken: and immediately all the doors were opened, and every one's bands were loosed. Acts 16:22

On one occasion, Paul was left for dead but the Breaker Anointing raised and healed him. He did not have to be hospitalized for three weeks or more.

And there came thither certain Jews from Antioch and Iconium, who persuaded the people, and, having stoned Paul, drew him out of the city, supposing he had been dead.

Howbeit, as the disciples stood round about him, he rose up, and came into the city: and the next day he departed with Barnabas to Derbe. Acts 14:19-20

"The Holy Spirit is a gentleman but His acts are not gentle".

For whether we live, we live unto the Lord; and whether we die, we die unto the Lord: whether we live therefore, or die, we are the Lord's. Romans 14:8

One is bound to wonder, what motivated the Prophets, Paul and the other Apostles to follow YHVH and lay down their lives for the gospel.

33 Who through faith subdued Kingdoms, wrought righteousness, obtained promises, stopped the mouths of lions,

34 Quenched the violence of fire, escaped the edge of the sword, out of weakness were made strong, waxed valiant in fight, turned to flight the armies of the aliens.

35 Women received their dead raised to life again: and others were tortured, not accepting deliverance; that they might obtain a better resurrection:

36 And others had trial of [cruel] mockings and scourgings, yea, moreover of bonds and imprisonment:

37 They were stoned, they were sawn asunder, were tempted, were slain with the sword: they wandered about in sheepskins and goatskins; being destitute, afflicted, tormented; Hebrews 11:33-37

That which was from the beginning, which we have heard, which we have seen with our eyes, which we have looked upon, and our hands have handled, of the Word of life; 1John 1:1,3; Acts 4:20

The Apostles came to a very vital conclusion concerning Jesus when they said;

"Lord, to whom shall we go? Thou hast the Words of eternal life." John 6:68

We must come to the conclusion that there is no one but Jesus and His Word is life and we have nowhere else to go but to Him.

And David came to Baalperazim, and David smote them there, and said, The LORD hath broken forth upon mine enemies before me, as the breach of waters. Therefore he called the name of that place Baalperazim. 2Samuel 5:20

"YHVH hath broken forth upon mine enemies like a mighty Tsunami" – EFOV.

David was a Statesman, and must defend his country. The State has the right to use every weapon of war to defend itself.

And it shall come to pass in that day, that his burden shall be taken away from off thy shoulder, and his yoke from off thy neck and the yoke shall be destroyed because of the anointing. Isaiah 10:27

How God anointed Jesus of Nazareth with the Holy Ghost and with power: who went about doing good, and healing all that were oppressed of the devil; for God was with him. Acts 10:38

The Spirit of the Lord (The Breaker) is upon me, because he hath anointed (**The Breaker anointing**) me to preach the gospel to the poor; he hath sent me to heal the brokenhearted, to preach deliverance to the captives, and recovering of sight to the blind, to set at liberty them that are bruised. Luke 4:18

The Covenant is the guarantor of the Breaker or the Violent Anointing.

*As for me, this is **my covenant** with them, saith the LORD; **My spirit that is upon thee, and my Words which I have put in***

thy mouth, *shall not depart out of thy mouth, nor out of the mouth of thy seed, nor out of the mouth of thy seed's seed, saith the LORD, from henceforth and forever.* Isaiah 59:21

Your spirit receives the charge as you pray in the Holy Ghost, and when fully charged up (critical mass), you detonate with Words or touch" causing healing and miracle explosion.

Anointing is the Spirit of YHVH upon us, ready to manifest as we charge up our spirit and speak His Words.

But ye, beloved, building up yourselves on your most holy faith, praying in the Holy Ghost, Jude 1:20

*He that speaketh in an unknown tongue **edifieth himself;** but he that prophesieth edifieth the church.* 1Corinthians 14:14

In Genesis, The Spirit of YHVH was incubating or hovering over the waters and YHVH spoke and the miracles of creation came into being. We see that the pattern or principle is – **The Spirit and The Word.**

So shall my Word be that goeth forth out of my mouth: it shall not return unto me void, but it shall accomplish that which I please, and it shall prosper in the thing whereto I sent it. Isaiah 55:11

The Spirit of YHVH speaks Words: "…they are spirit and life…" John.6:63; "… sharper than any two edged sword…" Hebrew 4:12; "… and shall prosper in the thing whereto I sent it…" Isaiah 55:11. The Word must grow mightily (speaking in tongues over it) and prevail or be executed in your life as you declare it.

Atomic Power With YeHoVaH (YHVH)

Power is in the splitting of the atom and Almighty power is in the splitting or breaking of the Word and it takes the Holy Spirit, The Breaker, to do it by revelation knowledge in our spirit as He broods over us and we echo His Words, manifestations come into being.

We should spend time in praying in the spirit over a scripture and meditating on it until critical mass is achieved and it is time for explosive manifestation of power.

*The spirit of man is **YHVH's nuclear reactor**, where the breaking of the Word (atom) and fusion take place to release spirit and life, while Words and touch are the conductors of His great power.*

For the Word of God is quick, and powerful, and sharper than any two edged sword, piercing even to the dividing asunder of soul and spirit, and of the joints and marrow, and is a discerner of the thoughts and intents of the heart. Hebrews 4:12

This Word of God, sharper than any two edged sword, spirit and life, with radiation power, with healing in His beams and wings is able to X-ray the thoughts of men, do intricate operation in the souls of men by lighting it up and dispelling the darkness of the soul (fear, guilt and shame); It makes alive the spirit and causes it to take its superior place to the soul. It does intricate operations in joints and marrows and in the vital organs and every cell of your body. It is surely active and powerful and the greatest power, greater than any atomic bomb man can conceive.

YHVH is the Consuming Fire and was in the fiery furnace with the three Hebrew men.

Psalm 91 declares that in the case of a massive bombing or atomic explosion, even if you are at ground zero, *a thousand will fall at thy side, ten thousand on your right hand but it will not affect you.*

You will go through the fire and it shall not kindle upon you.

We need power with YHVH, we need the Breaker or Violent Anointing for such a time as this as we are faced with the ***"Caliphate" and Rogue nations.*** Sons of God arise!!!

God operates in our spirit and not in our physical head and that is the reason we cannot see or hear God.

Our spirit is the candle (light bulb or lamp) of YHVH. YHVH's Spirit upon our spirit and His mouth in our mouth and we must speak as oracles of God.

"I release God's lightning rod to consume every rod of the wicked against you.

This is the day that the burdens and the yokes of the enemy shall be consumed by our God who is the Consuming Fire.

I release the soothing balm of Gilead on every joint. I rebuke the pain of arthritis, lupus etc.

I release the balm of Gilead – the precious blood of Jesus upon every sin stained soul for cleansing."

Sun of Righteousness: ***The Breaker Anointing, arise with healing in your beams and flares. Let flares jump on anyone that would read this book. Let the fire fall, let the fire fall. Amen.***

Elijah called fire from Heaven when he said *"…If I be a man of God…";* Elisha blinded a company of soldiers sent to apprehend him. Moses used various weapons of war to deliver the children of Israel out of bondage.

What are you capable of? You cannot and must not be a helpless pawn in the war of life. Quit ye like men.

Watch ye, stand fast in the faith, quit you like men, be strong. 1Corinthians 16:13.

Be Healed!!!

Be Healed!!!

YeHoVaH is your doctor and no copay required.

He declares "I am the YHVH that healeth thee." Not I was, not I will be but "I AM."

The testimonies abound of YHVH's ability to perform His Word. Jesus, or Yehoshua in Hebrew, which means YeHoVaH is Salvation implies YHVH, heals, protects, provides, saves etc.

The testimonies abound of YHVH's ability to perform.

Today Be Healed!!!; because:

1. **We can count on His faithfulness**
   God is not a man, that he should lie; neither the son of man, that he should repent: hath he said, and shall he not do it? or hath he spoken, and shall he not make it good? Numbers 23:19
2. **We can count on His oath.**
   *But because the LORD loved you, and because **he would keep the oath** which he had sworn unto your fathers, hath the LORD brought you out with a mighty hand, and **redeemed you out of the house of bondmen,** from the hand of Pharaoh King of Egypt.* Deuteronomy 7:8
   Sickness is servitude and the work of a hard taskmaster.
3. **We can count on His unfailing Word**
   *Blessed be the LORD, that hath given rest unto his people Israel, according to all that he promised: **there hath not failed one Word of all his good promise,** which he promised by the hand of Moses his servant.* 1Kings 8:56
4. **We can count on His ability.**

For I am the YHVH, I change not; therefore ye sons of Jacob are not consumed. Malachi 3:6
Jesus Christ the same yesterday, and today, and forever. Hebrews 13:8 5.

5. **We can count on YHVH's witnesses**
*Behold, I give unto you power to tread on serpents and scorpions, and **over all the power of the enemy: and nothing shall by any means hurt you.*** Luke 10:19
*Then Peter said, Silver and gold have I none; but such as I have give I thee: In the **name of Jesus Christ of Nazareth rise up and walk.*** Acts 3:6
"…they shall lay hands on the sick, and they shall recover…" Mark 16:18
*And I will pray the Father, and he shall give you another Comforter, that **he may abide with you for ever;*** John 14:16

YHVH wants to express His nature in you and through you. Jesus' ministry was a testimony of YHVH's willingness and ability to perform.

"Faith is in YHVH's Word, guaranteed or backed by His oath and His ability to perform".

*But without faith it is impossible to please him: for he that cometh to God must believe that He Is **(I AM),** and that he is a **rewarder (Performer)** of them that **diligently (confidently)** seek him.* Hebrews 11:6

*But let him ask in **faith, (absolute confidence in the I AM and His ability to PERFORM because of past testimonies)**, nothing wavering. For he that wavereth is like a wave of the sea driven with the wind and tossed. For let not that man think that he shall receive any thing of the Lord.* James 1:6,7

Then Jesus answering said unto them, Go your way, and

tell John what things ye have seen and heard; **how that the blind see, the lame walk, the lepers are cleansed, the deaf hear, the dead are raised, to the poor the gospel is preached.** Luke 7:22

On this day, I declare fibroids are healed, the barren become joyful mothers of children. The unmarried have their spouses and every manner of sicknesses and diseases are healed in Jesus Name. Amen!!!

Be Healed!!!

Be Healed 2!!!

Be Healed!!!

Then Jesus answering said unto them, "Go your way, and tell John what things ye have seen and heard"; how that the blind see, the lame walk, the lepers are cleansed, the deaf hear, the dead are raised, to the poor the gospel is preached. Luke 7:22

The above scripture was a testimony to John the Baptist about Jesus' mission as the Messiah.

On one occasion Jesus met with a leper who asked a pertinent question which some are still asking today and the response of Jesus should forever satisfy and settle the issue.

And there came a leper to Him, beseeching Him, and kneeling down to Him, and saying unto Him, "If thou wilt, thou canst make me clean." And Jesus, moved with compassion, put forth His hand, and touched him, and saith unto him, "I will; be thou clean". Mark 1:40,41

"I will", was and it is still the answer of Jesus concerning healing.

That it might be fulfilled which was spoken by Esaias the prophet, saying, Himself took our infirmities, and bare our sicknesses. Matthew 8:17

Jesus came to do the Father's will and He did nothing of His own, so healing is the Father's will.

For I came down from Heaven, not to do mine own will, but the will of Him that sent me.

And this is the will of Him that sent me, that everyone which seeth the Son, and believeth on Him, may have everlasting life:

and I will raise him up at the last day. John 6:38,40

Jesus said He came in the Father's name which is Yehoshua (YeHoVaH is Salvation). Jesus said "I have manifested thy name unto the men which Thou gavest me out of the world: Thine they were, and Thou gavest them me; and they have kept Thy Word. John 17:6

He also said "the Holy Spirit which the Father will send in my name" (The Father's name) John 14:26 and furthermore we are authorized to use the name in prayer and to make demands on Satan.

We here establish that the works are done in His Name; therefore healing is the will of God and it is in the Name.

Then Peter said, Silver and gold have I none; but such as I have, give I thee: In the name of Jesus the Messiah rise up and walk. Acts 3:6

We can declare that healing is in the will and final testament of Jesus and He is the administrator of His will today.

Jesus is the mediator of the New Testament (Will) and as we read the four gospels and the Acts of the Holy Spirit, we must reach the conclusion that YeHoVaH heals.

Why I must be healed now!!!

1. Satan, I am not in doubt of YHVH's faithfulness.
2. YHVH cannot lie.
3. YHVH watches over His Word to perform it.
4. I can count on YHVH's oath.
5. I have YHVH's testimonials in the gospel and Acts (His witnesses).
6. I know YHVH's will and testament concerning healing.
7. I know that Jesus died and rose again and is the

administrator of His will and testament.
8. I know healing is in Jesus' name and His name is not done away with.
9. Satan, these are grounds of faith without any shadow of a doubt and faith has not been done away with.
10. Healing has been paid for, signed, sealed and delivered. On these grounds I know healing is for me today and I believe it, know and receive it. I am HEALED now!!!

Be Healed 3!!!

Be Healed!!!

Faith has not been done away with, else no one can be saved. As long as people are saved through faith, healing, deliverance, protection, preservation, and the gifts of the Holy Spirit are available to all through faith.

The woman with the issue of blood touched the wings of His garment by faith in the Word of promise in Malachi 4:12 and because of her testimony, as many as touched Jesus, were made whole.

Jesus said to the woman "thy faith has made thee whole". Matthew 9:22. Your faith will still bring healing today. Amen.

And when the men of that place had knowledge of Him, they sent out into all that country round about, and brought unto Him all that were diseased; And besought Him that they might only touch the hem of His garment: and as many as touched were made perfectly whole. Matthew 14:35,36

And the whole multitude sought to touch Him: for there went virtue out of Him, and healed them all. Luke 6:19

And there sat a certain man at Lystra, impotent in his feet, being a cripple from his mother's womb, who never had walked: The same heard Paul speak: who steadfastly beholding him, and perceiving that he had faith to be healed, Said with a loud voice, Stand upright on thy feet. And he leaped and walked. Acts 14:8-10

And Peter said unto him, Aeneas, Jesus Christ maketh thee whole: arise, and make thy bed. And he arose immediately. Acts 9:34

Let's look at some more testimonies in Jesus' ministry:

When the even was come, they brought unto Him many that were possessed with devils: and He cast out the spirits with His Word, and healed all that were sick: Matthew 8:16

Now when the sun was setting, all they that had any sick with divers diseases brought them unto Him; and He laid His hands on every one of them, and healed them. Luke 4:40

And, behold, they brought to Him a man sick of the palsy, lying on a bed: and Jesus seeing their faith said unto the sick of the palsy; Son, be of good cheer; thy sins be forgiven thee….then saith He to the sick of the palsy, "Arise, take up thy bed, and go unto thine house." Matthew 9:2,6

And when Jesus departed thence, two blind men followed Him, crying, and saying, Thou Son of David, have mercy on us. And when He was come into the house, the blind men came to Him: and Jesus saith unto them, "Believe ye that I am able to do this?" They said unto Him, Yea, Lord. Then touched He their eyes, saying, "According to your faith be it unto you". Matthew 9:27-29

But when Jesus knew it, He withdrew Himself from thence: and great multitudes followed Him, and He healed them all; Matthew 12:15

My covenant will I not break, nor alter the thing that is gone out of my lips. Psalms 89:34

His covenant "I am YHVH that healeth thee or YHVH your Doctor." Exodus 15:26 stands sure.

For whosoever shall call upon the name of the Lord shall be saved (healed, delivered etc.). Roman 10:13

For the scripture saith, "Whosoever believeth on Him shall not be ashamed." Romans 10:11

1. The name of Jesus heals. Acts 3:6
2. Jesus Christ makes thee whole. Act 9:34
3. Faith to be healed. Acts 14:8-10; Matthew 9:22
4. Healed them all (you cannot be exempted). Luke 6:19
5. Diverse diseases. (yours included, HIV, cancer etc.) Luke 4:40
6. You shall not be ashamed. Romans 10:11
7. Whosoever means you. Romans 10:13

So, "Be Healed!!!"

So then faith cometh by hearing, and hearing by the Word (Rhema) of God. Romans 10:17

Read these scriptures over and over again and YHVH will say by Rhema (spoken Word) "You are healed!!!"

I have had YHVH the Doctor visit people at their homes at night during my Crusades and performed operations on them and healed them.

The Great Physician is here, the compassionate Jesus and He will visit and heal you.

"Be Healed!!!" IN JESUS NAME. AMEN!!!

Be Healed 4!!!

Be Healed!!!

The cessationists say that the days of miracles are gone. And since the greatest miracle is salvation (soteria) and those who have soteria are saved (sozo) this would imply that the cessationists can never be saved.

Soteria is a noun and sozo a verb. They are translated as salvation, saved, healing, wholeness, deliverance, provision, preservation etc.

It is a waste of time to argue about cessationism. What they need is a demonstration or a proof that Jesus of yesterday is the same today.

Why would a cessationist seek medical help? Just pray for them but above all else, let us demonstrate the gifts and the healing power of Jesus.

YHVH is interested in your three fold salvation in your spirit, soul and body.

And the very God of peace sanctify you wholly; and I pray God your whole spirit and soul and body be preserved blameless unto the coming of our Lord Jesus Christ. 1Thessalonians 5:23

Beloved, I wish above all things that thou mayest prosper and be in health, even as thy soul prospereth. 3John 2

Has the devil and his works ceased? Is God without a witness in the earth today? It is a resounding "NO".

YeHoVaH has forever settled the issue of our healing.

Surely He hath borne our griefs, and carried our sorrows: yet we did esteem Him stricken, smitten of God, and afflicted…..and with His stripes we are healed. Isaiah 53:4,5

That it might be fulfilled which was spoken by Esaias the prophet, saying, Himself took our infirmities, and bare our sicknesses. Matthew 8:17

Who His own self bare our sins in His own body on the tree, that we, being dead to sins, should live unto righteousness: by whose stripes ye were healed. 1Peter 2:24

These three scriptures tell us of:

1. The promise.

2. The fulfillment and

3. It is yours

What He took and what He bore for me, I need not take nor bear anymore. I am healed!!!

You are healed!; You are healed!!; You are healed!!!

Be Healed 5!!!

Be Healed!!!

Registered mail is a mail guaranteed to be delivered and signed off by the recipient. If you knew that the mail contained anthrax, a bomb etc., you will not accept nor open it.

YHVH has a mail delivery system and so does the devil.

Your healing has been signed, sealed and delivered by special delivery.

For God sent not His Son into the world to condemn the world; but that the world through Him might be saved (healed, delivered). John 3:17

In this was manifested the love of God toward us, because that God sent His only begotten Son into the world, that we might live through Him. 1John 4:9

YHVH took all your sickness and diseases and put it on Jesus the Messiah on the cross.

If one should ask you a question about "your" headache, cancer, diabetes, what would your answer be?

That it might be fulfilled which was spoken by Esaias the prophet, saying, Himself took our infirmities, and bare our sicknesses. Matthew 8:17

As a teenager, I read Ian Fleming's books and watched quite a lot of the James Bond movies. One common theme in all I have watched is that James Bond is captured and taken to the den or headquarters (HQ) of the wicked and there he destroys their works and escapes.

I have no doubt Mr. Ian Fleming got this theme from the works of Jesus.

All we like sheep have gone astray; we have turned everyone to his own way; and the YHVH hath laid on him the iniquity of us all. Isaiah 53:6

In this scripture "And I will put enmity between thee and the woman, and between thy seed and her seed; it shall bruise thy head, and thou shalt bruise his heel". Genesis 3:15, we see the promise of the deliverer.

In the betrayal and crucifixion of Jesus the Messiah, we see the part fulfillment of the above scripture "bruise His heel". YHVH baited the devil and he took it.

Which none of the princes of this world knew: for had they known it, they would not have crucified the Lord of glory. 1Corinthians 2:8

This brought Jesus, the Lamb of God, to the HQ of the enemy and on the third day, just before the third count and the bell, the Spirit of life (the resurrection power) came on Jesus the Ultimate Warrior and The Lion of Judah rose up. He was clothed with the armor of God, and He put off from Himself the wicked ones and left Satan and his hosts paralyzed as He put our infirmities and diseases on Satan.

There is a Lion in the Lamb of God, there is a Lion in His sheep, there is a Lion inside of you.

The Greater One is with you, for you and in you. The roar of a lion is in the midst of you.

Forasmuch then as the children are partakers of flesh and blood, He also Himself likewise took part of the same; that through death He might destroy him that had the power of death, that is, the devil; And deliver them who through fear of death were all their lifetime subjected to bondage. Hebrew 2:14,15

And having spoiled principalities and powers, He made a shew of them openly, triumphing over them in it. Colossians 2:15

14 Having cancelled and blotted out and wiped away the handwriting of the note (bond) with its legal decrees and demands which was in force and stood against us (hostile to us). This [note with its regulations, decrees, and demands] He set aside and cleared [j]completely out of our way by nailing it to [His] cross.

15 [God] disarmed the principalities and powers that were ranged against us and made a bold display and public example of them, in triumphing over them in Him and in it [the cross]. Colossians.2:14,15

Amplified For in that He himself hath suffered being tempted, He is able to succour (bring aid; help) them that are tempted. Hebrew 2:18

Help has come, aid has come. Satan's head has been crushed; Genesis 3:15 is forever settled.

Ye are of God, little children, and have overcome them: because greater is He that is in you, than he that is in the world. 1John 4:4

I know that, whatsoever God doeth, it shall be forever: nothing can be put to it, nor anything taken from it: and God doeth it, that men should fear before Him. Ecclesiastes 3:14

He that spared not His own Son, but delivered Him up for us all, how shall He not with Him also freely give us all things? Romans 8:32

Let the roar of the lion in you be heard. You are healed!!!

Be Healed!!!

Be Healed 6!!!

Be Healed!!!

Help has come, aid has come. Satan's head has been crushed. Genesis 3:15 is forever settled. You are healed!!!

By default: A situation or condition that obtains in the absence of active intervention. (thefreedictionary.com)

Our default setting was sin, sickness, diseases and death, then Jesus came and by the force of spiritual arms brought righteousness, healing, wholeness and abundant life.

Genesis 3:15 was forever settled, Satan, principalities and powers disarmed and this scripture fulfilled:

When a strong man armed keepeth his palace, his goods are in peace. But when a stronger than he shall come upon him, and overcome him, he taketh from him all his armour wherein he trusted, and divideth his spoils. Luke 11:21,22

Jesus took Satan's armor and he is therefore vulnerable to the least child of God who knows YHVH's active intervention and is wearing YHVH's armor.

Look unto Jesus and your new setting is healing and wholeness, but the moment you take your eyes off Jesus it defaults to bondage, sickness and disease.

Satan's salesmen

Satan's salesmen would gladly and have sold many a Timeshare in a Resort in Hell.

Jesus puts our sicknesses and diseases on Satan. Satan called his salesmen and put them into action to package sickness and diseases and send out by registered mail. He also sent salesmen to ring your door bell and sell you stuff, even in Churches.

I got this response to one of my posts on Facebook, and find also my reply:

Bill: God is not healing anyone today like it or not. Jesus would not heal Paul what makes you think anyone else is special.

Me: I agree with you "God is not healing anyone today" because "by His stripes they were healed". Know it, and the healing becomes a reality. Thanks Bill.

Bill and others like him want you back in the default settings.

The devil's agents want their commissions (copay) and for you to be in the most beautiful hospital in the world. Have you heard some ignorant person say "My cardiologist or specialist is world renowned". Who wants one in a Hospital Resort? If you do not accept healing from YHVH the Doctor, why would you seek healing from doctors?

Many ignorant ministers and salesmen for the Devil will tell you of Paul's thorn in the flesh. Paul had overabundance of revelation. Do you? The thorn was a messenger or salesman of Satan and YHVH told him just like He spoke to Moses "Why do you cry to me, what is in your hand?" Moses had the rod of authority and when he used it, deliverance came. YHVH said to Shaul (Paul), "My grace (All the resources of Heaven at your disposal) is sufficient for you" Use it.

Who hath believed our report? and to whom is the arm of the YHVH revealed? ...Surely He hath borne our griefs, and carried our sorrows: yet we did esteem Him stricken, smitten of God, and afflicted. But He was wounded for our transgressions; He was bruised for our iniquities: the chastisement of our peace was upon Him; and with His stripes we are healed. Isaiah 53:1,4,5

Plug into this grace that has been revealed. Use it!!! Be Healed!!!

Be Healed 7!!!

Be Healed!!!

When a strong man (Satan) armed keepeth his palace, his goods are in peace. But when a stronger (Jesus) than he shall come upon him, and overcome him, He taketh from him all his armour wherein he trusted, and divideth his spoils. Luke.11:21,22

In this was manifested the love of God toward us, because that God sent His only begotten Son into the world, that we might live through Him. 1John 4:9

What do you do when Satan's Salesmen knock on your door?

Satan sold Eve a Timeshare (Hotel Resort) outside Paradise, he made an effort to sell the world to the possessor of Heaven and Earth, Jesus the Messiah but failed woefully.

Did Jesus possess a special weapon that is not available to us today? The answer is a big NO. Jesus counteracted every sales pitch of Satan with "It is written"

"… it is written in the law of the LORD…". 2Chronicles 31:3

"… it is written in the law of Moses the man of God…". Ezra.3:2

"… It is written in the prophets,…" John 6:45

"… it is written in the book of Psalms…". Acts 1:20

If I may add:

"…it is written in the Gospels…"

"…it is written in the Epistles…"

"…it is written in the Revelation of Jesus the Messiah…"

Do you know what is written? And Jesus answered him, saying, "It is written, That man shall not live by bread alone, but by every Word of God." Luke 4:4

"…In the volume of the book it is written of me…" Hebrews 10:7.

What is written concerning you?

We having the same spirit of faith, according as it is written, I believed, and therefore have I spoken; we also believe, and therefore speak; 2Corinthians 4:13

But as it is written, Eye hath not seen, nor ear heard, neither have entered into the heart of man, the things which God hath prepared for them that love Him.

Jesus is the Word and He made sure He knew all that is written. He was a Specialist at His trade.

"…It is written, "That man shall not live by bread alone, but by every Word of God…" Luke 4:4

It is time to begin to say or prophesy to yourself what is written and not the test results or the doctor's report.

It is written, "YeHoVaH is my doctor."

It is written, "YHVH shall give his angels charge over me to keep me…"

It is written, "…YHVH sent ministering spirits to minister to me an heir of salvation…"

Speak to Satan's salesmen "…It is written…" and "…get thee behind me Satan…"

It is written "I am healed"; So, "Be Healed!!!"

Be Healed 8!!!

Be Healed!!!

Be Healed!!! and heal the sick is a command and a commission. If you are a believer, you are a Commissioned Officer by the Kingdom of Heaven. Your commission is to share the good news. YHVH wants to confirm His Word with signs and wonders.

And they went forth, and preached everywhere, the Lord working with them, and confirming the Word with signs following. Amen. Mark 16:20

The call or commission is to believers:

And these signs shall follow them that believe; In my name shall they cast out devils; they shall speak with new tongues; Mark 16:17

Heal the sick, cleanse the lepers, raise the dead, cast out devils: freely ye have received, freely give. Matthew.10:8

Many will say this verse refers to Apostles and I am not an Apostle. We find out that Peter and John used the name of Jesus which is also given to the believers to use.

Some will say "I don't have power and I am not holy". Hear what Peter had to say:

And when Peter saw it, he answered unto the people, Ye men of Israel, why marvel ye at this? or why look ye so earnestly on us, as though by our own power or holiness we had made this man to walk? Acts 3:12

For it is God which worketh in you both to will and to do of His good pleasure. Philippians 2:13

I would like to give an analogy:

A policeman had a quarrel with his wife just before she left for school to teach and their children attend the same school. The policeman, on his way to work, notices armed men (terrorists) sneaking into the school grounds.

What do you think he would do? If he is a Christian like many of us, I know what he would say and do. He would say I am a sinner, my heart condemns me, I just had a quarrel with my wife. I will be a hypocrite to shoot at the terrorists.

The policeman has been given authority (badge) and power (gun) and is commissioned to engage the enemy wherever found and will engage, but not the "Christian," who will allow the terrorist to have his way.

"as though by our own power or holiness we had made this man to walk" Acts 3:12

We allow sickness and disease, the works of the most wanted terrorists, Satan and his hosts to move freely to harass, torment and kill.

You might not have Apostolic Authority but you have the Believers Authority.

For it is God which worketh in you both to will and to do of his good pleasure. Philippians 2:13

It is YHVH's good pleasure to heal you and destroy all the works of the enemy and make you His battle axe and weapons of war. 1Jo 3:8; Jeremiah 51:20

Wherefore lift up the hands which hang down, and the feeble knees; And make straight paths for your feet, lest that which is lame be turned out of the way; but let it rather be healed. Hebrews 12:12,13

Let no one cross your path without you doing something about their condition.

Samson's ability was YHVH's ability working in him and the moment the Spirit left, he could do nothing; for there are no great men of God but the great God working in man and that includes YOU.

Be Healed!!! and Heal others by the great YHVH in you.

Be Healed 9!!!

Be Healed!!!

Bless the LORD, O my soul, and forget not all His benefits:

1. Who forgiveth all thine iniquities;
2. Who healeth all thy diseases;
3. Who redeemeth thy life from destruction;
4. Who crowneth thee with lovingkindness and tender mercies;
5. Who satisfieth thy mouth with good things;
6. So that thy youth is renewed like the eagle's.
7. The LORD executeth righteousness and judgments for all that are oppressed." Psalm 103:2-6

This is a Psalm worthy of our daily meditation.

I have learned that Chevron Oil Company Nigeria Ltd has a very great benefits and retirement benefits plan. I personally know that Nigerian National Petroleum Corporation (NNPC) has a great benefit plan also.

Many CEOs of big corporations in America have benefits that are three times or more, bigger than their salaries.

People know every inch of their benefits and use them. Child of God, YHVH has not left you without benefits.

The Psalmist is here pleading with his soul "forget not all his benefits".

I came across a family, who have airline benefits to fly for peanuts all over the world, but never left Texas. I would that someone give me such benefits, as an Evangelist.

I have come today to plead with you, along with the Psalmist, not to forget all the benefits that belong to every child of God.

Sins forgiven, great health plan, absolutely wonderful plans that includes protection from accidents, Boko Haram, ISIL, bombs, bullets, acid, plane or train crash etc.

Furthermore, we have favor plan and I love this one "Who satisfieth thy mouth with good things" : which implies satisfaction in silver, gold, raiment, houses, cars, good food etc.

You are also endowed with a youthful life to enjoy all these benefits. YHVH also wants to arise as God of battles to fight for you.

Be delivered from the spirit of blindness and let the rod of the oppressor be broken over your life.

Be Healed!!! and begin to enjoy the benefits YHVH has provided for you.

Please share this book or buy and give out as gifts and bless others.

"Be Healed!!!"

Be Healed 10!!!

Be Healed!!!

Blessed be the Lord, who daily loadeth us with benefits, even the God of our salvation (healing, deliverance, prosperity, preservation) Selah - (Pause and think about it). Psalms 68:19

What shall I render unto the LORD for all his benefits toward me? Psalms 116:12

Thou preparest a table before me in the presence of mine enemies: Thou annointest my head with oil; my cup runneth over. Psalm 23:5

He suffered no man to do them wrong: yea, He reproved kings for their sakes; Psalms 105:14

YHVH is mindful of you.

The LORD hath appeared of old unto me, saying, Yea, I have loved thee with an everlasting love: therefore with loving kindness have I drawn thee. Jeremiah 31:3

We have had unscriptural teachers and we have been taught lots of invalid beliefs.

YHVH wants to perform His Word in your life today.

Begin to think, dream, speak, see, meditate on the Word of God and YHVH will restore the years.

Car loads of benefits are coming your way. Hallelujah!!!

And I will restore to you the years that the locust hath eaten, the cankerworm, and the caterpillar, and the palmerworm, my great army which I sent among you. Joel 2:25;

And daily load you with car loads of benefits:

Health and more.

Dare to believe and dream : "Benefits, benefits, benefits, benefits, benefits,";

Think: "Benefits, benefits, benefits, benefits, benefits, benefits, benefits";

Speak: Benefits, benefits, benefits, benefits, benefits, benefits, benefits;

See: Benefits, benefits, benefits, benefits, benefits, benefits, benefits.

Amen!!!

YHVH will deliver!!! Be Healed!!! Amen!!!

Be Healed 11!!!

Be Healed!!!

Has God changed?. God has not changed. When men prayed for the sick and people still died, they created instead out of their experience the tradition and doctrine of extreme unction: anointing for death. When men because of lack of consecration prayed and no visible signs, wonders and miracles, they came up with the doctrine that the days of signs, miracles and wonders ended with the Apostles.

Many say today that tongues have ceased and prophecy ceased because they have not experienced it. Others preach doctrines based on their dreams and visions, which are flawed.

To the law and to the testimony: if they speak not according to this Word, it is because there is no light in them. Isaiah 8:20

He brought them forth also with silver and gold: and there was not one feeble person among their tribes. Psalms 105:37

Whither shall we go up? Our brethren have discouraged our heart, saying, "The people is greater and taller than we; the cities are great and walled up to Heaven; and moreover we have seen the sons of the Anakims there. Deuteronomy 1:28

Strengthen ye the weak hands, and confirm the feeble knees. Isaiah 35:3

In the days of David, the children of Israel cowered because of the giant Goliath but David had a different spirit like Joshua and Caleb and slew the giant. David and his men encountered four other giants the sons of Goliath and slew them.

There is no giant today that cannot be slain, no mountain that cannot be moved by those with another spirit (The Spirit of YHVH).

While others walk by sight, we must walk by faith. Nothing is impossible!!!

Does YHVH have answers to the digital age and would be anti-Christ system? YES!, YES!!, YES!!!

For, behold, YHVH will come with fire, and with His chariots like a whirlwind, to render His anger with fury, and His rebuke with flames of fire. Isaiah 66:15

And of the angels he saith, "Who maketh his angels spirits, and His ministers a flame of fire. Hebrew 1:7

Today, scientists are scared of coronary mass ejections (CMEs). "The geomagnetic storm that results from CME-magnetosphere interactions can muck up all kinds of technology that we rely upon in modern life." (World Science Festival).

Elijah called down fire from Heaven. We can do the same today as fire is the antidote to every weapon at the disposal of the devil and the anti-Christ.

Become a flame of fire, become wind. A whirlwind of fire is the choice weapon we need for this end time.

YHVH still shelter's by the pillar of fire. YHVH zaps every disease known or imagined electronic diseases or pestilence with fire. Amen.

The god of science, or the computer god the Millennials trust in, is no match to the flames of fire, the Sons of Fire (Boanerges).

The wind bloweth where it listeth, and thou hearest the sound thereof, but canst not tell whence it cometh, and whither it goeth: so is every one that is born of the Spirit. John 3:8

For God hath not given us the spirit of fear; but of power, and of love, and of a sound mind. 2Timothy 1:7 I speak to the mountain that confronts you "Be moved from your life" and I speak unto you "Be Healed by the flame of fire!!!".

Be Healed!!!

Be Healed 12!!!

Be Healed!!!

Do It Yourself (DIY)

What will you do if there is no Pastor to pray for you or your family?

What will you do if all your Pastor does is to bury the dead or hold funeral services?

What will you do? What will you do?

We are in an era where Corporations have copyrights, trade secrets and propriety stuffs and these same spirits are in the Churches.

Many ministers want to be superstars and never duplicate themselves and die with their anointing.

John G Lake taught people how to heal the sick so did Charles and Frances Hunter.

Jesus did not rebuke Peter, when he requested to walk on the water. He said to him "Come." Jesus is saying to you today, "Come".

The disciple is not above his master, nor the servant above his lord. It is enough for the disciple that he be as his master, and the servant as his lord. Matthew 10:24,25

Verily, verily, I say unto you, He that believeth on me, the works that I do shall he do also; and greater works than these shall he do; because I go unto my Father. John 14:12

"We are all called to be disciples and believers and you do not need a title to heal the sick".

There is no great man of God who heals the sick, but YHVH heals through them as He will you. YHVH is looking for Do It Yourselfers, simple folks to do His work today.

Follow these teachings and you will awaken to who YHVH has made you to be.

Start today and lay hands on yourself and family and command sickness by name or symptom to go, in Jesus Name. Amen.

And these signs shall follow them that believe; In my name shall they cast out devils; they shall speak with new tongues; …they shall lay hands on the sick, and they shall recover. The Lord working with them, and confirming the Word with signs following. Amen. Mark 16:17,18,20

Do It Yourself and be Be Healed Today!!!

Be Healed 13!!!

Be Healed!!!

Bless the LORD, O my soul, and forget not all His benefits: Who forgiveth all thine iniquities; who healeth all Thy diseases; ....The LORD executeth righteousness and judgment for all that are oppressed. Psalms 103:2,3,6

I would want to render vs.6 this way:

"YHVH executeth Justice. Justice demands that the oppressed be set free and restitution be made to him and that the oppressor be punished by a Heavenly Judicial order and executed by Heavens agents: Angels or believers for All that are oppressed (violated, defrauded, wronged)". EFOV.

Homosexuals have come a long way from being treated as insane to having a voice in America today and within the same time period the Church has been degraded.

The government of this world knows that the title deed of this world is to be given to the Saints. Satan is afraid of you, governments are afraid of you and world religions and caliphates are scared of you. Saints of God arise and know the things that have been freely given to you.

Until the Ancient of days came, and judgment was given to the saints of the most High; and the time came that the saints possessed the Kingdom. Daniel 7:22.

But the saints of the most High shall take the Kingdom, and possess the Kingdom forever, even for ever and ever. Daniel 7:18

26 But the judgment shall sit, and they shall take away his dominion, to consume and to destroy it unto the end.

27 And the Kingdom and dominion, and the greatness of the Kingdom under the whole Heaven, shall be given to the people of the saints of the most High, whose Kingdom is an everlasting Kingdom, and all dominions shall serve and obey Him. Daniel 7:26,27

Sin and diseases have been condemned by the Supreme Court of Heaven.

Defend the poor and fatherless: do justice to the afflicted and needy. Deliver the poor and needy: rid them out of the hand of the wicked.

I have said, Ye are gods; and all of you are children of the most High. Psalms 82:3,4,6

To execute upon them the judgment written: this honour have all his saints. Praise ye the LORD. Psalms 149:9

Do not live and die like chicks, like a mere mortal man. Let us arise today and begin to set one man, one family free from the tyranny and yoke of bondage.

Rise up and be healed!!!

Sickness and diseases, the Supreme Court of Heaven has passed judgment on you. I make demand on you to restore health to the oppressed and restitution be paid. In Jesus name.

Be Healed from All Diseases!!!

I _____ of City _____

State _____ by Heavens Court order I am FREE and HEALED NOW

Signed, Sealed, delivered and executed this _____

Day of _____ 20____

Received by:_____ Sign _____

Date_____

Heavens Agent: Enahoro Francis Ovienmhada

Be Healed 14!!!

Be Healed!!!

The Enforcer: a person, especially a public official, who enforces laws, regulations, rules, or the like. (dictionary.com)

Jesus was an official of Heaven who enforced the rule of Heaven on earth.

The Judge of Heaven and Earth has passed judgement that need to be enforced.

Over and over again in the New Testament we see Jesus enforcing the rule of the Kingdom.

And, behold, there was a woman which had a spirit of infirmity eighteen years, and was bowed together, and could in no wise lift up herself. And when Jesus saw her, He called her to Him, and said unto her, Woman, thou art loosed from thine infirmity. And He laid His hands on her: and immediately she was made straight, and glorified God. And ought not this woman, being a daughter of Abraham, whom Satan hath bound, lo, these eighteen years, be loosed from this bond on the Sabbath day?

Luke 13:11-13,16

After these things the Lord appointed other seventy also, and sent them two and two before His face into every city and place, whither He Himself would come. …And into whatsoever city ye enter, and they receive you, eat such things as are set before you: And heal the sick that are therein, and say unto them, "The Kingdom of God is come nigh unto you". And the seventy returned again with joy, saying, "Lord, even the devils are subject unto us through Thy name." "Behold, I give unto you power to tread on serpents and scorpions, and over all the power of the enemy: and nothing shall by any means hurt you." Luke 10:1,8,9, 17,19

And as ye go, preach, saying, The Kingdom of Heaven is at hand. Heal the sick, cleanse the lepers, raise the dead, cast out devils: freely ye have received, freely give. Matthew 10:7,8

And He said unto them, when ye pray, say, "Our Father which art in Heaven, Hallowed be Thy name. Thy Kingdom come. Thy will be done, as in Heaven, so in earth. Luke 11:2

The policeman does not call to find out if he has to arrest an offender of the law or someone with a warrant over their head. He enforces the warrant and makes an arrest. Christians should stop praying to God about the devil and his agents but enforce the law: arrest, bind, cast and destroy their works.

And I will give unto thee the keys of the Kingdom of Heaven: and whatsoever thou shalt bind on earth shall be bound in Heaven: and whatsoever thou shalt loose on earth shall be loosed in Heaven. Matthew 16:19

The name of Jesus has been conferred on us, we have authority (badge) and we have power (gun), lets enforce healing.

"To execute upon them the judgment written: this honour have all his saints. Praise Ye the LORD." Psalms 149:9

Be Healed!!!

Be Healed 15!!!

Be Healed!!!

And they went forth, and preached everywhere, the Lord working with them, and confirming the Word with signs following. Amen. Mark 16:20

Manifestations come as you go forth. Many want to feel the anointing first before they go. There is a group I am aware of who are waiting for special anointing and they have waited forever and till date I have not seen any manifestations.

For many years I had Sunday Night Healing Service. After a while, I stopped and for about six months did not pray for any sick person. I attended a service where I was invited to lay hands on a few sick folks and I felt empty. Now I am back to holding Healing Meetings at the House of Healing first and second Thursdays of the month and there is a flow of the healing anointing again.

In the ministry of Charles and Frances Hunter, amazing results and manifestations were abundant as ordinary folks in pairs healed the sick. It is not titles that we need but obedience to the command of God and enforcement of the mandate "Thy will be done on earth as it is in Heaven."

There were amazing results in John G. Lake's Ministry, in five years they had over 100,000 confirmed healing in Spokane Washington. He raised up Divine Healing Technicians or shall we say believers. Today, Curry Blake is in charge of the ministry and the tradition of ordinary folks healing the sick continues and many dead have been raised.

I make bold as to say that if Charles and Frances Hunter, John G. Lake, Curry Blake, Apostle Johnson Suleman and any known ministers can heal the sick, YOU can". Yes, YOU can!!!

You speak to the mountain (diseases: cancer, pain etc.) to go in the name of Jesus and it leaves your hands into the hands of Jesus.

In the name of Jesus Christ of Nazareth, rise up and walk. Acts 3:6 is not a prayer but an exercise of authority and dominion.

And whatsoever ye shall ask (DEMAND) in my name, that will I do, that the Father may be glorified in the Son. If ye shall ask (DEMAND) anything in my name, I will do it. John 14:13,14

"Please could you let him go" is asking, but when you say "Let him go", it is a demand and exercise of authority.

You have authority and power, use it and Jesus will confirm with signs and wonders following Amen.

The real terrorists, claiming thousands of lives are not Boko Haram, ISIL etc. Not wars, like WW1 or WW2 or any of the recent wars but heart disease, cancer, diabetes, kill more people in a year than all these wars combined.

We may add millions of babies killed each year through abortion and you want to call Boko Haram or ISIL murderers?

Submit yourselves therefore to God. Resist the devil, and he will flee from you. James 4:7

Be Healed!!! and Heal the Sick!!!

Be Healed 16!!!

Be Healed!!!

Idolatry has been a plague in the African society and as such they idolize men of God. When you idolize a man of God, you have put him on a pedestal, an elite status, a giant and you look at yourself as a grasshopper. I know of several groups who have made GIANTS out of men of God and have remained grasshoppers to this day. Americans love idols, too.

We should have the "no limitations" Spirit in Joshua and Caleb, "no limitations" and not the spirit of the majority with grasshopper mentality.

I would state categorically that, "No man of God should be your Capstone, but every man of God should be your stepping stone."

Whatever a man of God can do, you can do also. This is not to disrespect, or dishonor them, be it far from that, but find out what they did to get there, do the same and YHVH, who is no respecter of persons, will get you there.

It is time to kill the giant of limitation that wants to make you or has made you a grasshopper. There is a stone from the sling of prayer to take it down and you have to walk away from such a group.

The goal of Jesus was not to be the only Superstar but to make every believer one. If Jesus were an African say a Yoruba, when Peter asked to walk on the water, His response would have been "O mo egbe?" interpreted, would mean we are not in the same league; and in Pidgin English, "you nor know your mate?"; As an American, "what the heck".

Verily, verily, I say unto you, He that believeth on Me, the works that I do shall he do also; and greater works than these shall he do; because I go unto my Father. John 14:12

Whose report will you believe? Being like Jesus or being a grasshopper?

There is a man of God, I recently came across on YouTube, Apostle Johnson Suleman and I will encourage everyone to watch him, light your candle and run with it. He lit his candle by learning the principles of spiritual operation from the late Archbishop Benson Idahosa. The grasshoppers are still grasshoppers today, but he has stepped up. In this race, overtaking is allowed, as our goal is to be like Jesus.

David's mighty men were ordinary folks who became renowned. David is a very good example of a real Pastor/Shepherd, that raised up mighty men and not grasshoppers.

Pastors should know their limitations and allow the people to manifest their endowments by the Spirit of God. You are still the pastor and sign the checks. Moreover, it is YHVH's business and not your LLC. These phrases will keep the Holy Spirit away and make grasshoppers of men. "My Church" "I am THE pastor". The Church belongs to Jesus and He is THE Pastor. Please raise up disciples for Jesus.

My favorite authors: Andrew Murray, E. W Kenyon, Smith Wigglesworth. John G. Lake, Mary Woodworth Etter, Kenneth Hagin, Kathryn Khulman, and Enahoro Francis Ovienmhada.

On YouTube: E. W Kenyon, John G. Lake, Kenneth Hagin and Kathryn Khulman and you can find me on Facebook: Francis Enahoro; Arizona WildFire ; Sun of Righteousness Ministries and Healing The Children's Bread. Also, on YouTube : Thehealingwings; Francis Enahoro and Hardcore Christianity.

https://www.youtube.com/watch?v=8wyLlsa7SpM

Let us go and do the greater works, light your candles and go get the terrorists (demons, sickness and diseases).

"Be Healed!!!" and "Heal the Sick!!!

Be Healed 17!!!

Be Healed!!!

And Caleb stilled the people before Moses, and said, Let us go up at once, and possess it; for we are well able to overcome it. Numbers 13:30

We need to rent our clothes like Caleb and weep, with so much unbelief in the Church. We and our seed will not die in the wilderness but possess our possession. We shall possess the enemies' gate.

Forty five years later Caleb said "Now therefore give me this mountain", Joshua 14:12

And Caleb drove thence the three sons of Anak, Sheshai, and Ahiman, and Talmai, the children of Anak. Joshua 15:14

Caleb requested for the mountain, the land of the giants and defeated them.

"There is no giant so big, no mountain so large that faith in Christ Jesus cannot conquer."

"Raise up the banner of YHVH

Raze down every stronghold

Bulldoze every mountain

Bind every strong man

Possess the gates of the enemies."

There is an old, old refrain:

We are able to go up and take the country

To possess the land from Jordan to the sea

Though the giants may be on our way to hinder

God will surely give us victory.

Kittie L. Suffield 1922

I would like us to pray these prayer points:

1. Come against the spirit of discouragement.
2. Come against the spirit of limitations.
3. Come against the spirit of fear.
4. Come against the spirit of unbelief.
5. Come against giant and grasshopper mentality (inferiority complex).
6. Pray for the spirit of boldness. I will not die like a mere man.
7. YHVH light my candle.
8. YHVH let my light shine.
9. I break forth and I breakthrough into the realms of God. Behold, what manner of love the Father hath bestowed upon us, that we should be called the sons of God: therefore the world knoweth us not, because it knew Him not. Beloved, now are we the sons of God, and it doth not yet appear what we shall be: but we know that, when He shall appear, we shall be like Him; for we shall see Him as He is. 1John 3:1, 2

    Herein is our love made perfect, that we may have boldness in the day of judgment: because as He is, so are we in this world. 1John 4:17

Let us rise up and do the works of Jesus: Heal the sick, cast out demons and raise the dead. Yes, you can!; Yes, you can!!; Yes, you can!!!

"Be Healed!!!" and "Heal the Sick!!!"

Be Healed 18!!!

Be Healed!!!

The devil has tricked some into believing that there is no God, taught others that God no longer heals. To some, he questions "If God loves you why does He not heal you?" To others, yet again the devil tells them God is teaching them a lesson by their sicknesses.

For those who are supposed to be taught lessons through their sickness, why do they seek medical help instead of learning the lessons?

Woe to them that go down to Egypt (World) for help; and stay on horses, and trust in chariots, because they are many; and in horsemen, because they are very strong; but they look not unto the Holy One of Israel, neither seek YHVH! Isaiah 31:1

Some trust in chariots, and some in horses: but we will remember the name of YHVH our God. Psalm 20:7

It is time to break every tombstone and memorial the devil has placed in the minds of the people.

God is a good God and the devil is bad and evil.

One of the earliest memory verses my son learnt was "O taste and see that the LORD is good: blessed is the man that trusteth in Him." Psalms 34:8

Many have not tasted nor put their trust in YHVH.

The thief (Satan) cometh not, but for to steal, and to kill, and to destroy: I (Jesus) am come that they might have life, and that they might have it more abundantly. John 10:10

John G. Lake once said "I am tired of doctors, medicine and the devil" and when his consecration was complete, the evil disease that had ravaged him most of his life, left him.

The woman with the issue of blood was tired of doctors, insurance companies, the pharmaceuticals and said "...If I can but touch...". Will you trust and touch Him today?

I can hear cries and the desperation of many today, but the Great Physician, our great and compassionate High Priest, the sympathizing Jesus is still the same. God is bigger than your problems, bigger than the mountains, bigger than the giants.

I would like to refer us to the prayers in "Be Healed 17!!!" Pray it until every hold of the enemy is broken. The gates of hell shall not prevail against you.

Thus saith the LORD; cursed be the man that trusteth in man, and maketh thy flesh his arm and whose heart departeth from the LORD. "...Blessed is the man that trusteth in the LORD, and whose hope the LORD is..." Jeremiah 17:5,7

Thou wilt keep Him in perfect peace, whose mind is stayed on Thee: because He trusteth in thee. Isaiah 26:3

I will go before thee, and make the crooked places straight: I will break in pieces the gates of brass, and cut in sunder the bars of iron. Isaiah 45:2

7 Lift up your heads, O ye gates; and be ye lift up, ye everlasting doors; and the King of glory shall come in.

8 Who [is] this King of glory? The LORD strong and mighty, the LORD mighty in battle.

9 Lift up your heads, O ye gates; even lift [them] up, ye everlasting doors; and the King of glory shall come in.

10 Who is this King of glory? The LORD of hosts, he [is] the King of glory. Selah. Psalms 24:7-10

The gates of unbelief, fear, discouragement, inferiority complex etc. be lifted up and YHVH, the Lord of Hosts steps in and becomes your Salvation & Healing.

I slay every giant, bulldoze every mountain and command every problem "Be vanquished!!!"

"There is no hospital beautiful enough for those that trust in YHVH.

There is no doctor great enough, but YHVH the Doctor.

No anesthesia good enough, but to be put under the influence of the Holy Spirit.

No surgeon's knife, but the Word that is sharper than any two edged Sword and that leaves no scars."

Be Healed!!!

Be Healed 19!!!

Be Healed!!!

Therefore, I take pleasure in infirmities (want of strength and capacity requisite), in reproaches, in necessities, in persecutions, in distresses for Christ's sake: for when I am weak, then am I strong. 2 Corinthians 12:10

"Infirmities" in the above scripture relates to: want of strength and capacity requisite; to bear trials and troubles and he concludes with "when I am weak, then I am strong". This implies he draws from the Grace of YHVH.

This brings us to Paul's thorn in the flesh, which was well defined as a messenger of Satan to buffet him. Now, Paul prayed three times and YHVH spoke and said, "My grace is sufficient for you". Weak – Strong; Read Sea - Rod.

YHVH told Paul to use the resources, Grace has provided. It was never sickness or diseases.

Why are you looking for reasons or excuses to be sick? Why are you looking for a point of view that would keep you in your condition?

Suffering persecution is part of Christianity, and though we appear to be at ease in America, there are many martyrs of Christ in many parts of the world.

But he shall receive an hundredfold now in this time, houses, and brethren, and sisters, and mothers, and children, and lands, with persecutions; and in the world to come eternal life. Mark 10:30

Persecutions, afflictions, which came unto me at Antioch, at Iconium, at Lystra; what persecutions I endured: but out of them all the Lord delivered me. 2Timothy 3:11

Many are the afflictions of the righteous: but the LORD delivereth him out of them all. Psalm 34:19.

If afflicted pray… sick call the elders James 5:13

Lack of knowledge of the Will of God and wisdom is the reason for often misinterpreted scriptures.

"The devil wants you sick and seeking the help of some fifth columnist preachers and teachers to keep you sick, beats my imagination".

And there he found a certain man named Aeneas, which had kept his bed eight years, and was sick of the palsy. And Peter said unto him, Aeneas, Jesus Christ maketh thee whole: arise, and make thy bed. And he arose immediately. Acts.9:33,34

Jesus saith unto him, Rise, take up thy bed, and walk. John 5:8

To you I say "Jesus makes you whole. Rise, leave your hospital bed and go home"

Be Healed!!!

Be Healed 20!!!

Be Healed!!!

6 For whom the Lord loveth He chasteneth (for a child to learn or be instructed through discipline/affliction), and scourgeth every son whom He receiveth.

7 If ye endure chastening, God dealeth with you as with sons; for what son is he whom the Father chasteneth not?

8 But if ye be without chastisement, whereof all are partakers, then are ye bastards, and not sons. Hebrews 12:6-8

Though He were a Son, yet learned He obedience by the things which He suffered; Hebrews 5:8

But the God of all grace, who hath called us unto His eternal glory by Christ Jesus, after that ye have suffered a while, make you perfect, stablish, strengthen, settle you. 1Peter 5:10

Are they ministers of Christ? (I speak as a fool) I am more; in labours more abundant, in stripes above measure, in prisons more frequent, in deaths oft. Of the Jews five times received I forty stripes save one. Thrice was I beaten with rods, once was I stoned, thrice I suffered shipwreck, a night and a day I have been in the deep; in journeyings often, in perils of waters, in perils of robbers, in perils by mine own countrymen, in perils by the heathen, in perils in the city, in perils in the wilderness, in perils in the sea, in perils among false brethren; In weariness and painfulness, in watchings often, in hunger and thirst, in fastings often, in cold and nakedness.

2Corinthians 11:23-27 Henceforth there is laid up for me a crown of righteousness, which the Lord, the righteous judge, shall give me at that day: and not to me only, but unto all them also that love His appearing. 2Timothy 4:8

We have the Bill of Rights, here in America.

We have the right of free speech and to protest but not to turn it into violence at which time the State will put you in the slammer.

You might well be an American journalist and slam the President here in the USA, but you cannot go to North Korea and slam their President and claim first amendment, you will be forgotten in jail, if not killed.

There is Heaven's Bill of Rights that belong to every righteous citizen of the Kingdom.

The Redemptive Names reveal what YHVH will do for every righteous citizen of the Kingdom. As long as you are within the boundaries of the Kingdom, you are protected.

Rights are being eroded in America. It was not too long ago the Supreme Court struck down the Marriage Act and redefined marriage for Americans. About 40 years ago the right to kill babies was enacted called abortion.

These acts of the Judiciary constitute rebellion against God and be it known that every act of disobedience against YHVH shall be punished. When the rumblings start, only those who have stayed within the confines of YHVH's law will be protected.

A thousand shall fall at thy side, and ten thousand at thy right hand; but it shall not come nigh thee. Psalm 91:7

Elijah confronted Ahab and it ended up in the Mount Carmel Showdown.

Persecutions, testings and trials are coming to America and we would be required to operate in the fringe. Radical Christianity is standing for the truth against all odds, but we are not helpless pawns as the weapons of our warfare are not carnal.

That it might be fulfilled which was spoken by Esaias the prophet, saying, Himself took our infirmities, and bare our sicknesses. Matthew 8:17

YHVH does not put sickness and diseases on people He takes them away.

Every good gift and every perfect gift is from above, and cometh down from the Father of lights, with whom is no variableness, neither shadow of turning. James 1:17

Be Healed!!!

Be Healed 21!!!

Be Healed!!!

We are in a digital age and have to face digital sicknesses and diseases.

We are bombarded with Electro Magnetic Frequencies (EMF's), microwaves from cell phone towers, high tension lines and various electronic gadgets.

These waves and radiation cause motion sickness, insomnia, cancer, mental confusion, and death to name a few.

We are in an atomic age, and at a time when nuclear disasters will happen more frequently plus the fear of dirty bombs and the certain nuclear war.

There have been at least five nuclear accidents to date and notable ones are Chernobyl in 1986, Fukushima Nuclear Disaster in 2011 and some incidents in the USA.

Surveillance is now key to governments and America has overnight, become a police state. There are eyes and ears in the gadgets and utilities we have in our homes. There are eyes in the sky, video cameras on our roads and cameras everywhere.

Is there protection available to the believer in Jesus Christ from these destructive waves and radiations? Also from the Evil Eye?

And the LORD will create upon every dwelling place of mount Zion, and upon her assemblies, a cloud and smoke by day, and the shining of a flaming fire by night: for upon all the glory shall be a defense. And there shall be a tabernacle for a shadow in the daytime from the heat, and for a place of refuge, and for a covert from storm and from rain. Isaiah 4:5,6;

But we have to be washed by YeHoVaH.

The Children of Israel in their forty years journey in the wilderness were protected from deadly rays from the desert sun by the Pillar of cloud by day.

Psalm Ninety-one, talks of protection when a thousand fall at our side and ten thousand on our right hand. It starts with "He that dwelleth in the secret place of the most High shall abide under the shadow of the Almighty." Psalms 91:1

Putting on the whole armor of God and quenching all the fiery darts of the enemy is available to the believer.

No weapon that is formed against thee shall prosper; and every tongue that shall rise against thee in judgment thou shalt condemn. This is the heritage of the servants of the LORD, and their righteousness is of Me, saith the LORD. Isaiah 54:17

In the book Things Fall Apart by Chinua Achebe, it is written about Eneke the bird "Men have learned to shoot without missing their mark and I have learned to fly without perching on a twig." – An Igbo proverb.

If demons have gone digital and governments have gone digital, why is the Church still in the analog mode?

There was a transportation system available to Phillip; Jesus walked through the midst of those who took Him to the brow of the mountain to kill Him. We must become Super-Digital and be above all the powers of the enemy.

There was a wave or virtue that flowed out of Peter so that the sick were laid on the street and the least thing that happened was his shadow healed the sick. Handkerchiefs and aprons from Paul carried virtue that healed the sick and cast out demons.

The wind bloweth where it listeth, and thou hearest the sound thereof, but canst not tell whence it cometh, and whither it goeth: so is every one that is born of the Spirit. John 3:8

He sent his Word, and healed them, and delivered them from their destructions Psalm 107:20

Welcome to the super-digital Age of believers. Be Healed!!!

Be Healed 22!!!

Be Healed!!!

"…The inhabitant shall not say I am sick…" Isaiah 33:24

Sin and sickness is prevalent in the "Church". It has been found that on the average 80% of a congregation are sick.

Many in this group claim they are "Christians" implying that they have believed in the saving of their souls.

Two issues confront us here: If they are saved, why are they sick? Is salvation only for the soul and not for the body?

The problem, I see is with centuries of denominationalism and orthodoxy. They taught the people about sin and getting to Heaven and were incapable of dealing with sickness and disease but rather taught that these were part of the dealings of God.

The scriptures say "Let every man who experiences orthodoxy be a lie and let God be true." EFOV.

From the mouth of two or three witnesses shall every truth be established.

Who forgiveth all thine iniquities; who healeth all thy diseases; Psalms 103:3

And the inhabitant shall not say, I am sick: the people that dwell therein shall be forgiven their iniquity. Isaiah 33:24

In the Old Testament (OT), we have these two witnesses, now let us see what the New Testament (NT) has to say:

But that ye may know that the Son of man hath power on earth to forgive sins, (then saith He to the sick of the palsy,) Arise, take up thy bed, and go unto thine house. Matthew 9:6

Afterward Jesus findeth him in the temple, and said unto him,

Behold, thou art made whole: sin no more, lest a worse thing come unto thee. John 5:14

The ministry of Jesus was to bring the good news (gospel) of the Kingdom of God: forgiveness of sin, healing of the body and the destruction of every work of the enemy. The disciples were commissioned to do the same.

And he sent them to preach (the good news) the Kingdom of God, and to heal the sick. Luke 9:2

And as ye go, preach, saying, The Kingdom of Heaven is at hand. Heal the sick, cleanse the lepers, raise the dead, cast out devils: freely ye have received, freely give. Matthew 10:7,8

Then Philip went down to the city of Samaria, and preached Christ (Messiah) unto them. For unclean spirits crying with loud voices, came out of many that were possessed with them: and many taken with palsies, and that were lame, were healed. And there was great joy in that city. Acts 8:5-8

And the inhabitant shall not say, I am sick: the people that dwell therein shall be forgiven their iniquity. Isaiah 33:24

"The I am that YHVH says I am, that I am"

Should be well established in our souls and as citizens of the Kingdom, we cannot say "I am sick".

YHVH who forgives my iniquities is the One that heals my diseases and I declare: I am forgiven, I am healed.

Orthodox: (of a person or their views, especially religious or political ones, or other beliefs or practices) conforming to what is generally or traditionally accepted as right or true; established and approved. (google.com)

Be Healed!!! I am Healed!!!

Be Healed 23!!!

Be Healed!!!

Then came the disciples to Jesus apart, and said, Why could not we cast him out? And Jesus said unto them, Because of your unbelief: for verily I say unto you, If ye have faith as a grain of mustard seed, ye shall say unto this mountain, Remove hence to yonder place; and it shall remove; and nothing shall be impossible unto you. Matthew 17:19,20

Now Jesus had commissioned them to:

Heal the sick, cleanse the lepers, raise the dead, cast out devils: freely ye have received, freely give. Matthew 10:8

This was an apparent failure on their part and Jesus' rebuke was stern in Matthew 17:17 and I will like to give the EFO Version.

O generation without trust in God who turn away at the least resistance and want to be propped up always; when are you going to take responsibility and do the works? EFOV

In one of Kenneth Hagin's meetings he was met with apparent failure in dealing with demons after he had seen Jesus in a vision and was instructed on how to cast them out. In the face of apparent defeat, Jesus appeared and was very stern "I said in My name demons will go!" and the fourth time Jesus jabbed His finger at him and said emphatically "Yes, but I said the demons will go!". He got it and the demons came out, the man was healed and "if" the badge of doubt "See if you can stoop over…." was forever dealt with.

"…and nothing shall be impossible unto you…" Matthew 17:20

"Unbelief is sin! To doubt YHVH's ability to heal you is to have faith in the ability of the devil to keep you sick".

Jesus could do no mighty works in His home town because of unbelief but only laid His hands on a few with minor ailments.

Unbelief was the reason for forty years wanderings of the Israelites in the wilderness. Fear, doubt and unbelief are tools of the devil to keep you from your miracles and the Church needs a cure from them.

Be Healed!!!

Be Healed 24!!!

Be Healed!!!

Then came the disciples to Jesus apart, and said, Why could not we cast him out? And Jesus said unto them, Because of your unbelief: for verily I say unto you, If ye have faith as a grain of mustard seed, ye shall say unto this mountain, Remove hence to yonder place; and it shall remove; and nothing shall be impossible unto you. Matthew 17:19,20

Now Jesus had commissioned them to:

Heal the sick, cleanse the lepers, raise the dead, cast out devils: freely ye have received, freely give. Matthew 10:8

This was an apparent failure on their part and Jesus' rebuke was stern in Matthew 17:17 and I will like to give the EFO Version.

O generation without trust in God who turn away at the least resistance and want to be propped up always; when are you going to take responsibility and do the works? EFOV

In one of Kenneth Hagin's meetings he was met with apparent failure in dealing with demons after he had seen Jesus in a vision and was instructed on how to cast them out. In the face of apparent defeat, Jesus appeared and was very stern "I said in My name demons will go!" and the fourth time Jesus jabbed His finger at him and said emphatically "Yes, but I said the demons will go!". He got it and the demons came out, the man was healed and "if" the badge of doubt "See if you can stoop over…." was forever dealt with.

"…and nothing shall be impossible unto you…" Matthew 17:20

"Unbelief is sin! To doubt YHVH's ability to heal you is to have faith in the ability of the devil to keep you sick".

Jesus could do no mighty works in His home town because of unbelief but only laid His hands on a few with minor ailments. Unbelief was the reason for forty years wanderings of the Israelites in the wilderness.

Fear, doubt and unbelief are tools of the devil to keep you from your miracles and the Church needs a cure from them.

Be Healed!!!

Be Healed 25!!!

Be Healed!!!

And when the disciples saw him walking on the sea, they were troubled, saying, It is a spirit; and they cried out for fear. But straightway Jesus spoke unto them, saying, Be of good cheer; it is I; be not afraid. Matthew 14:26,27

But when he saw the wind boisterous, he was afraid; and beginning to sink, he cried, saying, Lord, save me. And immediately Jesus stretched forth His hand, and caught him, and said unto him, O thou of little faith, wherefore didst thou doubt? Matthew 14:31

We have previously established the fact that Jesus does not want to be the only Superstar but invites all to walk on the water.

Though we try to emphasize the fact of Peter doubting and beginning to sink, we must all come to the conclusion that the man Peter walked on the sea.

And he said, Come. And when Peter was come down out of the ship, he walked on the water, to go to Jesus. Matthew 14:29

The miracle of walking on the sea started but was terminated because of fear, unbelief and doubt as he was challenged by a violent wind. There is a wind that wants to challenge and to violently change the course of our healing and miracles. However, there is a breath, a puff of wind from our mouth that can stop any violent challenge.

But what saith it? The Word is nigh thee, even in thy mouth, and in thy heart: that is, the Word of faith, which we preach; Roman 10:8 All Peter needed to do was to speak the Word of faith "Violent wind, hush!!! Jesus said Come."

"Faith that started the miracle was on the grounds of the Words of Jesus and faith that sustains a miracle to conclusion rest on the same Words".

I married a little over thirty two years ago and we prayed for three years for a child and finally the miracle started.

One night, a cat came to the window of the room where my wife was sleeping and started crying like a baby. The sweet Holy Spirit caused me to start speaking in tongues in my sleep. I gradually came into consciousness speaking in tongues, stood up and rebuked the cat in the name of Jesus and I saw it run away. The cat was white with brown spots.

About a week later, an owl physically attacked my wife and the baby started moving in the womb. I came home and saw my wife on her knees praying. She turned to me and told me what had happened. I asked my wife if witchcraft had started the miracle? If they did not, then they cannot terminate it. I asked her to stand up and placed my hands on her belly and I said "Peace, be still" and the miracle was sustained.

Being confident of this very thing; He which hath begun a good work in you will perform it until the day of Jesus Christ: Philippians.1:6

Our eyes must be single and we must look unto Jesus, the author and finisher of our faith.

Who art thou, O great mountain? Before Zerubbabel thou shalt become a plain: and he shall bring forth the headstone thereof with shoutings, crying, Grace, grace unto it. Zechariah 4:7

Now pray and declare:

Who art thou, O boisterous (violent) wind, great mountain before (name), you shall be a plain and I shall bring forth the headstone, finishing stone, completion stone, crowning stone to my healing and miracle. In Jesus' name. Amen.

Be Healed!!!

Be Healed 26!!!

Be Healed!!!

And he did not many mighty works there because of their unbelief. Matthew 13:58

One can only wonder how many blind, lame, barren, tormented and insane were left without a miracle because of unbelief. We must seek the cure for unbelief.

God is able to do exceeding abundantly above all that we ask or think. The Scripture works, and you have to work it.

And they came to Him, and awoke Him, saying, "Master, Master, we perish". Then He arose, and rebuked the wind and the raging of the water: and they ceased, and there was a calm. And He said unto them, "Where is your faith?" And they, being afraid wondered, saying one to another, "What manner of man is this? For He commandeth even the winds and water, and they obey Him. Luke 8:24,26; Mark 4:39,40

Here, the disciples were challenged by wind and raging water and Jesus was teaching them an object lesson. He expected them to use their faith. We cannot be sitting ducks but must confront with spiritual weapons everything that confronts us. The contention of the enemy is to keep you away from your healing, health, miracle and destination.

Give no place to the devil, resist the devil and he will flee from you.

Don't allow your healing, miracle be terminated because the situation seems worse after prayers. Do not walk by sight but by faith.

Doctors report, bring or produce the reaction of fear to those who are not grounded in the Word. Those who are grounded respond to, and not react to, the report.

God does not intend for us to fail in any situation as a result of fear, doubt or unbelief. "I can do all things … all things are possible … all things you ask in prayers… Ask what you will …"; are Words of YHVH that cannot fail.

I am passing over to the other side, storm or no storm because I have the Word that tells me so. Fear breeds unbelief. Jesus was teaching them an object lesson to always stand on YHVH's unfailing Word of promise. He expected them to pass the test by stilling the storm.

"There is faith-Word that stills every storm of life".

Mark 11:23 – Say to this mountain of storm, fear or doubt and it shall be moved.

Mark.16:18 - Lay hands on the sick and they shall…, not might; He who has started a good thing in you, will finish it. If you receive a part of your miracle, persist until the whole miracle comes.

I am not moved by what I see. I am not moved by what I feel. I am moved only by the Word of faith. "If thou shall say.." (Adapted)

Be Healed!!!

Be Healed 27!!!

Be Healed!!!

Abraham had doubt and got a child by Hagar but YHVH had a cure for his doubt and changed his name from Abram to Abraham. Abraham was now forced to introduce himself as Abraham (the father of many nations) and caused men to prophesy unto him each time they called him Abraham – the father of many nations.

Abraham was forced to use faith helpers, "so shall your seed be" by looking up at the stars at night and sands under his feet as he walked on, and hearing the promise – father of many nations.

Faith comes by hearing and seeing and speaking, the promise.

Believe the Word, speak the Word, hear the Word and see the Word, no matter what confronts you, you will come out victorious.

And this is the confidence that we have in Him, that, if we ask anything according to His will, He heareth us: And if we know that He hears us, whatsoever we ask, we know that we have the petitions that we desired of Him. 1John 5:14,15

Beloved, if our heart condemns us not, then have we confidence toward God. And whatsoever we ask, we receive of Him, because we keep His commandments, and do those things that are pleasing in His sight. 1John 3:21, 22

Do not give place to the devil through fear, doubt and unbelief as they come to challenge your confidence towards God.

God is faithful, His Word true, He is able and I believe that "There shall be a Performance!!!"

Be Healed!!!

Be Healed 28!!!

Be Healed!!!

And the people spoke against God, and against Moses, "Wherefore have ye brought us up out of Egypt to die in the wilderness? For there is no bread, neither is there any water; and our soul loatheth this light bread. Numbers 21:5

"When you speak against the Word of God, you are speaking for the enemy, with the enemy and by the enemy".

3 And did all eat the same spiritual meat;

4 And did all drink the same spiritual drink: for they drank of that spiritual Rock that followed them: and that Rock was Christ.

5 But with many of them God was not well pleased: for they were overthrown in the wilderness. 1Corinthians 10:3-5

Looking and speaking according to the facts or circumstances that confront you and not according to the Word of God will cause an overthrow of your healing or miracle.

"… nevertheless at thy Word …" "…come walk on the water…".

Our reason and ability to do anything must be according to His Word or at His instance.

For unto us was the gospel preached, as well as unto them: but the Word preached did not profit them, not being mixed with faith in them that heard it. Hebrews 4:2

Fear, doubt and unbelief will cause to come to you what you do not want.

Call them well, cleansed, healed the way Jesus sees it, calling the things that are not as though they were. All power has been given unto Jesus, let us "go ye" therefore and manifest His power and bring Him glory.

Call upon me and I will answer you: delays are no reason to doubt. God heard Daniel the first day, but it took twenty-one days for the angel to get through because of resistance of the enemy. Do not leave your post or address through fear, doubt or unbelief, the answer is on its way.

Fear, doubt and unbelief are the enemies of your own creation. Kill them.

You are licensed to kill fear, doubt and unbelief!!! Use lethal force!!!

I believe God!!!

Be Healed!!!

Be Healed 29!!!

Be Healed!!!

For by one offering He hath perfected forever them that are sanctified (separated from the profane). Hebrews 10:14 Hagiazo (Sanctified) implies one who is separated from the profane: to defile, pollute, to make common.

Jesus' offering has separated you from sickness and diseases which defile and pollute your body and wants to make you common. Your body is the temple of God and is not common. YHVH must be glorified in your body because you are the temple of the Most High God.

Christ hath redeemed us from the curse of the law, being made a curse for us: for it is written, Cursed is every one that hangeth on a tree: Galatians 3:13

Curses are despicable, so are sicknesses and diseases and Jesus says "No more despicable and profane in your body". This is the key into His redemption for you.

According as His divine power hath given unto us all things that pertain unto life and godliness, through the knowledge of Him that hath called us to glory and virtue. 2 Peter 1:3

He that believeth hath!!!

It is done!!! It is forever settled!!!

Be Healed!!!

Be Healed 30!!!

Be Healed!!!

In those days was Hezekiah sick unto death. And Isaiah the prophet the son of Amoz came unto him, and said unto him, Thus saith the LORD, Set thine house in order: for thou shalt die, and not live. Isaiah 38:1-5

This was the sentence of the God of Justice that judged righteously based on present circumstances in Hezekiah's life.

Verse 2. Then Hezekiah turned his face toward the wall, and prayed unto the LORD,

3 And said, Remember now, O LORD, I beseech thee, how I have walked before thee in truth and with a perfect heart, and have done [that which is] good in thy sight. And Hezekiah wept sore.

However, Hezekiah decided to change his present condition or circumstances that warranted the judgement of YHVH, in humility and repentance.

Verse 4 Then came the Word of the LORD to Isaiah, saying,

5 Go, and say to Hezekiah, "thus saith the LORD, the God of David thy Father, I have heard thy prayer, I have seen thy tears: behold, I will add unto thy days fifteen years."

The judgement on Hezekiah was reversed and so will yours, if you will humble yourself and pray.

Beloved, if our heart condemn us not, then have we confidence toward God. 1John 3:21

I would want us to check if there is condemnation in our hearts because we cannot approach unto God with filthy hearts and hands.

And whatsoever we ask, we receive of Him, because we keep His commandments, and do those things that are pleasing in His sight. 1John 3:22

Be Healed 31!!!

Be Healed!!!

Doctors, medicine and healing

Doctors and medicines have important roles today for so many reasons. As a little boy growing up in Lagos Nigeria, my father would talk to us about preventative medicine. He had a big poster in our dining room and made every one of us children, to memorize it.

It read:

"Cleanliness is a good habit of keeping oneself and surroundings clean and tidy". Heart disease, high blood pressure, cancer and other chronic conditions are off springs of obesity and obesity is the daughter of your lust (meat, poultry, dairy, packaged and refined food).

In Nigeria, the fad of "Cash Madam" and pot belly (evidence of good living they claim) is really cashing in on sickness and disease.

Developing good eating habits and exercise regime is vital to our overall health.

Many are the afflictions of the righteous: but the LORD delivereth him out of them all. Psalm 34:19

Affliction: evil, distress, adversity and not sickness and disease.

It is quite interesting today that many Christians eat pigs which they call by the beautiful names of ham and bacon. A pig is a waste management animal. So also are prawns, lobsters which are sea roaches, cat fish etc.

Some Christians lay claim on the vision Peter had on the roof top and say, "...that which God has cleansed call thou not unclean...". Acts 10:10-21

It is only a reference to the Gentiles coming to the fold and not to feed your lust.

Know ye not that your bodies are the members of Christ? Shall I then take the members of Christ, and make them the members of an harlot? God forbid. What? Know ye not that your body is the temple of the Holy Ghost which is in you, which ye have of God, and ye are not your own? For ye are bought with a price: therefore glorify God in your body, and in your spirit, which are God's. 1 Corinthians 6:14, 19, 20

Fornication is lust of the flesh as much as the lust for strange and unclean flesh like the pig. Pig was used to defile the temple of God and still defiles today. We frown at the drunkard and forget about the glutton.

We may not agree on this issue, however, we are brethren and I will be the first to agree with you that forbidden things are sweet.

And the very God of peace sanctify you wholly; and I pray God your whole spirit and soul and body be preserved blameless unto the coming of our Lord Jesus Christ. 1Thessalonians 5:23

I would like to appeal to you not to cut your life short because of unhealthy appetites.

Let not sin therefore reign in your mortal body, that ye should obey it in the lusts thereof. Neither yield ye your members as instruments of unrighteousness unto sin: but yield yourselves unto God, as those that are alive from the dead, and your members as instruments of righteousness unto God. Roman 6:13

For sin shall not have dominion over you: for ye are not under the law, but under grace. What then? Shall we sin, because we are not under the law, but under grace? God forbid. 1Corinthians 6:15

Eating unhealthy flesh, has been implicated over 35,000 cases of colon cancer in Britain every year and about half of them die.

The statistics of new cases of cancer in Nigeria is about 102,100 per year and about 71,600 deaths per year according to the International Agency for Research on Cancer (IARC). It appears that very high death rates of about 70% are recorded in less developed regions. When you add heart disease, diabetes and hypertension plus poverty, African nations are in very grave danger of extinction. It was also reported that there were 14.1 million new cases of cancer worldwide in 2012 and 8.2 million deaths in the same year.

The above information is for us to be proactive concerning our healing and health.

Eat right and develop your faith everyday by hearing the Word of God and by your confessions.

For with the heart man believeth unto righteousness; and with the mouth confession is made unto salvation (healing, deliverance, protection, preservation). Romans 10:10

My father would make us wash the open drain we call gutter in front of our home every Saturday and use IZAL, a disinfectant. He said "mosquitos breed in these open drains and where do we think would be their first point of call? It would be the nearest home to the drain."

Though it was the government's responsibility to clean the drains and keep them flowing, they are usually stagnant and they hardly ever showed up for months and maybe years.

We also used insecticide in our home. The phrase "go and flit the house" was in common usage. Flit was the brand name of the insecticide and there was a flit gun. De-worming was common practice then and I can remember some of the disgusting medicines like Mist Alba and Cascara Sagrada liquid. He also prepared some herbal stuff for us to take. In my growing up years, I never saw my father at home sick and not go to work. The only time was when he had chicken pox.

Why we need doctors and medicine today:

1. We do not practice preventative medicine.
2. We go to the hospital when the sickness or disease has advanced.
3. We do not eat right and must pay the consequences.
4. We need doctors for emergencies.
5. We need doctors because of religion: a form of godliness that denies the power of God.
6. We need doctors because pastors are powerless to help.
7. We need doctors because of lack of faith.

I believe in miracles, I believe in healing. However, many people have died with make beliefs. They would not go to the hospital or use medication as prescribed.

He that believeth hath. You cannot have faith and not possess. You do not build your faith at the point of need, when it is too late.

Faith is not emotions or psyching oneself up. Faith comes by hearing, seeing, meditating and confessing the Word of God. It is built up on a daily basis and when there is a demand on it, it responds with healing and health that amazes doctors.

If you do not have faith, take your doctor's prescription while you are eating right and building your faith.

A Pastor should not to tell you to quit your medication. When you are healed, your doctor will be the one to give you a clean bill of health and discontinue your medication.

I am not a fan of pharmaceuticals. If you are eating right, using preventative medicine or herbs, exercising and building up your faith, you will have no need of them, with their too many to name side-effects. Until then, follow your doctor's orders.

The lepers were healed by Jesus but they had to go to the priest for check-ups and be declared cleansed. When the woman with the issue of blood was healed, the plague stopped. The man born blind could see and you cannot argue with the testimony of a dead man at a meal table (Lazarus). The case of the healing of the man born lame at the gate beautiful was well described by the Sanhedrin with these Words, "…that a notable miracle has been done, we cannot deny it…"

You will know when your healing or miracle comes and have no need of presumption.

But ye, beloved, building up yourselves on your most holy faith, praying in the Holy Ghost, Jude 1:20

Let us pray:

My body is the temple of God and not the breeding ground for sickness and disease. YHVH is my Doctor and my defense. I release the fire of God to burn any evil seed in my body. No evil arrow shall prosper in my body because it is written: "…No weapon formed against me shall prosper…" and I condemn every evil pronouncement against me, in Jesus Name. Amen.

Suicide

Hello friends, it is absolutely unacceptable to suffer and die from diabetes, cancer and heart disease. It is a criminal offense, it is suicide. Lust (meat, chicken, milk) like the monkey's hand in the banana jar is killing you. Cancer, heart disease, diabetes and other chronic illnesses can be reversed by eating vegetables, raw vegetables.

Kill cancer cells and reverse diabetes with nuts, fruits, vegetables and whole grains.

Moringa is a leaf that God has made available in most parts of the world and it is loaded with vital nutrients for the body. Everyone suffering from diabetes that I introduced to the use of Moringa, are very thankful today. Moringa trees should be planted in every home in Africa, India, and wherever Moringa trees grow.

You don't need to go under the Surgeon's knife if you use your forks today to eat vegetables.

Please watch the movie Forks over Knives and stay on top of your health.

Why commit suicide? Why dig your grave with your teeth? Please don't die, many are counting on you: spouse, children and parents. This is the generation we are told that will not live as long as their parents and probably be buried by their parents. Change this trend today and live.

More than two-thirds of U.S. adults are overweight or obese (Ogden et al., 2014)

Eat the Word of God today and live.

Thy Words were found, and I did eat them; and thy Word was

unto me the joy and rejoicing of mine heart: for I am called by thy name, O LORD God of hosts. Jeremiah 15:16

Healing is YeHoVaH's covenant with His people. He also gave us healing herbs. You can eat your way to life or eat your way to death.

Colorectal cancer is the third leading cause of cancer in males and fourth in females in the U.S. -(www.medicinenet.com)

The cost of ignorance is massive, and can cost you your life. I am told that a simple colonoscopy and clipping of polyps can save you from colon cancer. It is highly recommended that Black folks should start the test when they turn 40 years and White folks at 50 years. Have you had yours? Set up an appointment today.

Get the polyps now and do not wait until the curb becomes a lion and eat you up. Do not feed cancer with these: Meat, Poultry and Dairies and refined foods.

Doctors will tell you about the color of your "dump" but I say unto you:

"If it is not green you are eating your way to death."

I can testify of my friend who was going blind and his feet tingling because of diabetes. He made the choice of a vegetarian diet and amazed his doctor. He is free from diabetes.

I can testify of friends and families who actively took Moringa and are free today from type 2 diabetes.

I can testify at this writing that I have lost 20 lbs. and enjoy a good sleep and I am healthy.

Go green today!!! "Build your faith !!!" and "Be Healed!!!"

My Prayer/Confessions

Blessed be the God and Father of our Lord Jesus Christ, who hath blessed us with all spiritual blessings in Heavenly places in Christ: Ephesians 1:3

16 I cease not to give thanks for you, making mention of you in my prayers;

17 That the God of our Lord Jesus Christ, the Father of glory, may give unto you the spirit of wisdom and revelation in the knowledge of Him:

18 The eyes of your understanding being enlightened; that ye may know what is the hope of His calling, and what the riches of the glory of His inheritance in the saints,

19 And what [is] the exceeding greatness of his power to us-ward who believe, according to the working of His mighty power,

20 Which He wrought in Christ, when He raised him from the dead, and set [him] at His own right hand in the Heavenly [places],

21 Far above all principality, and power, and might, and dominion, and every name that is named, not only in this world, but also in that which is to come: Ephesians 1:16-21

14 For this cause I bow my knees unto the Father of our Lord Jesus Christ,

15 Of whom the whole family in Heaven and earth is named,

16 That He would grant you, according to the riches of His glory, to be strengthened with might by His Spirit in the inner man;

17 That Christ may dwell in your hearts by faith; that ye, being rooted and grounded in love,

18 May be able to comprehend with all saints what [is] the breadth, and length, and depth, and height;

19 And to know the love of Christ, which passeth knowledge, that ye might be filled with all the fulness of God. Ephesians 3:14-19

9 And this I pray, that your love may abound yet more and more in knowledge and [in] all judgment;

10 That ye may approve things that are excellent; that ye may be sincere and without offence till the day of Christ;

11 Being filled with the fruits of righteousness, which are by Jesus Christ, unto the glory and praise of God. Philippians 1:9-11 9 For this cause we also, since the day we heard [it], do not cease to pray for you, and to desire that ye might be filled with the knowledge of His will in all wisdom and spiritual understanding;

10 That ye might walk worthy of the Lord unto all pleasing, being fruitful in every good work, and increasing in the knowledge of God;

11 Strengthened with all might, according to his glorious power, unto all patience and longsuffering with joyfulness;

12 Giving thanks unto the Father, which hath made us meet to be partakers of the inheritance of the saints in light:

13 Who hath delivered us from the power of darkness, and hath translated [us] into the Kingdom of His dear Son:

14 In whom we have redemption through His blood, [even] the forgiveness of sins:

15 Who is the image of the invisible God, the firstborn of every creature:

16 For by Him were all things created, that are in Heaven, and that are in earth, visible and invisible, whether [they be] thrones, or dominions, or principalities, or powers: all things were created by

Him, and for Him:

17 And He is before all things, and by Him all things consist.

18 And He is the head of the body, the church: who is the beginning, the firstborn from the dead; that in all [things] He might have the preeminence. Colossians 1:9-18

For the Word of God is quick, and powerful, and sharper than any two-edged sword, piercing even to the dividing asunder of soul and spirit, and of the joints and marrow, and is a discerner of the thoughts and intents of the heart. Hebrews 4:12

Healing Scriptures

Memorize, make Confessions of and Use as Prayer Points

The Principle

(As it is written, I have made thee a father of many nations) before him whom he believed, even God, who quickeneth the dead, and calleth those things which be not as though they were. Roman 4:17

For verily I say unto you, "That whosoever shall say unto this mountain, Be thou removed, and be thou cast into the sea; and shall not doubt in his heart, but shall believe that those things which he saith shall come to pass; he shall have whatsoever he saith. Mark 11:23

But what saith it? The Word is nigh thee, even in thy mouth, and in thy heart: that is, the Word of faith, which we preach; Roman 10:8

As for me, this is my covenant with them, saith the LORD; My spirit that is upon thee, and My Words which I have put in thy mouth, shall not depart out of thy mouth, nor out of the mouth of thy seed, nor out of the mouth of thy seed's seed, saith the LORD, from henceforth and forever. Isaiah 59:21

"…And the Spirit of God moved upon the face of the waters. And God said …" Genesis 1:2,3

My heart is inditing a good matter: I speak of the things which I have made touching the King: My tongue is the pen of a ready writer. Psalm 45:1

"The faithful and persistent application of scriptures will bring amazing results and excellence in ministry that generations to come will talk about."

Healing Scriptures

And forgive us our debts, as we forgive our debtors. Matthew 6:12

For, if our heart condemns us, God is greater than our heart, and knoweth all things. Beloved, if our heart condemns us not, then have we confidence toward God. 1 John 3:20, 21

And hope maketh not ashamed; because the love of God is shed abroad in our hearts by the Holy Ghost which is given unto us. Roman. 5:5

Who His own self bare our sins in his own body, on the tree that we, being dead to sins, should live unto righteousness: by whose stripes ye were healed. 1Peter 2:24

Likewise reckon ye also yourselves to be dead indeed unto sin, but alive unto God through Jesus Christ our Lord. Roman 6:11

For He hath made Him to be sin for us, who knew no sin; that we might be made the righteousness of God in Him. 2 Corinthians 5:21

Let us therefore come boldly unto the throne of grace that we may obtain mercy, and find grace to help in time of need. Hebrews 4:16

He sent his Word, and healed them, and delivered them from their destructions. Psalms 107:20

Ye are of God, little children, and have overcome them: because greater is He that is in you, than he that is in the world. 1John 4:4

And they overcame him by the blood of the Lamb, and by the word of their testimony; and they loved not their lives unto the death. Revelation 12:11

The thief cometh not, but for to steal, and to kill, and to destroy: I am come that they might have life, and that they might have it more abundantly. John 10:10

It is the spirit that quickeneth; the flesh profiteth nothing: the words that I speak unto you, they are spirit, and they are life. John 6:63

My son, attend to my Words; incline thine ear unto my sayings. Let them not depart from thine eyes; keep them in the midst of thine heart: For they are life unto those that find them, and health to all their flesh. Proverbs 4:20-22

So mightily grew the Word of God and prevailed. Acts 19:20

And Moses was an hundred and twenty years old when he died: his eye was not dim, nor his natural force abated. Deuteronomy 34:7

There shall no evil befall thee, neither shall any plague come nigh thy dwelling: For He shall give His angels charge over thee, to keep thee in all thy ways. Psalm 91:10-11

In the way of righteousness is life; and in the pathway thereof there is no death. Proverb 12:28

What shall we then say to these things? If God be for us, who can be against us? He that spared not his own Son, but delivered Him up for us all, how shall He not with Him also freely give us all things? Rom 8:31

Nay, in all these things we are more than conquerors through Him that loved us. Roman 8:37

That it might be fulfilled which was spoken by Esaias the prophet, saying, Himself took our infirmities, and bare our sicknesses. Matthew 8:17

Christ hath redeemed us from the curse of the law, being made a curse for us: for it is written, Cursed is everyone that hangeth on a tree: Galatians 3:13

For verily I say unto you, That whosoever shall say unto this mountain, Be thou removed, and be thou cast into the sea; and shall not doubt in his heart, but shall believe that those things which he saith shall come to pass; he shall have whatsoever he saith. Mark 11:23

And the Lord said, "If ye had faith as a grain of mustard seed, ye might say unto this sycamine tree, Be thou plucked up by the root, and be thou planted in the sea; and it should obey you." Luke 17:6

For as the Father hath life in Himself; so hath He given to the Son to have life in Himself; John 5:26

The wind bloweth where it listeth, and thou hearest the sound thereof, but canst not tell whence it cometh, and whither it goeth: so is everyone that is born of the Spirit. John 3:8

Who His own self bare our sins in His own body on the tree that we, being dead to sins, should live unto righteousness: by whose stripes ye were healed. 1Peter 2:24

I beseech you therefore, brethren, by the mercies of God, that ye present your bodies as a living sacrifice, holy, acceptable unto God, which is your reasonable service. And be not conformed to this world: Be ye transformed by the renewing of your mind, that ye may prove what is good, and acceptable, and perfect, will of God. Roman 12:1,2

At that day ye shall know that I am in my Father, and ye in Me, and I in you. John 14:20

What? Know ye not that your body is the temple of the Holy

Ghost which is in you, which ye have of God, and ye are not your own?

For ye are bought with a price: therefore glorify God in your body, and in your spirit, which are God's. 1 Corinthians 6:19,20

And I will give unto thee the keys of the Kingdom of Heaven: and whatsoever thou shalt bind on earth shall be bound in Heaven: and whatsoever thou shalt loose on earth shall be loosed in Heaven. Matthew 16:19

And whatsoever ye shall ask in my name, that will I do, that the Father may be glorified in the Son. John 14:13

Who hath delivered us from the power of darkness, and hath translated us into the Kingdom of His dear Son: In whom we have redemption through His blood, even the forgiveness of sins. Colossians 1:13,14

And God blessed them, and God said unto them, be fruitful, and multiply, and replenish the earth, and subdue it: and have dominion over the fish of the sea, and over the fowl of the air, and over every living thing that moveth upon the earth.

And God saw everything that He had made, and, behold, it was very good. And the evening and the morning were the sixth day. Genesis 1:28,31

Wherefore lay apart all filthiness and superfluity of naughtiness, and receive with meekness the engrafted Word, which is able to save your souls. James 1:21

He sent his Word, and healed them, and delivered them from their destructions. Psalms 107:20

He that keepeth his mouth keepeth his life: but he that openeth wide his lips shall have destruction. Proverbs 13:3

And Jesus said unto them, "Because of your unbelief: verily I say unto you, "If ye have faith as a grain of mustard seed, ye shall say unto this mountain, Remove hence to yonder place; and it shall remove; and nothing shall be impossible unto you. Matthew 17:20

For the law of the Spirit of life in Christ Jesus hath made me free from the law of sin and death. Roman 8:2

Therefore, brethren, we are debtors, not to the flesh, to live after the flesh. For if ye live after the flesh, ye shall die: but if ye through the Spirit do mortify the deeds of the body, ye shall live. Romans 8:12, 13

A man shall be satisfied with good by the fruit of his mouth: and the recompense of a man's hands shall be rendered unto him. Proverbs 12:14

A sound heart is the life of the flesh: but envy the rottenness of the bones. Proverb 14:30

I am in them, and thou in Me, that they may be made perfect in one; and that the world may know that thou hast sent Me, and hast loved them, as thou hast loved Me. John 17:23

In whom ye also are built together for an habitation of God through the Spirit. Ephesians 2:22

For if by one man's offence death reigned by one; much more they which receive abundance of grace and of the gift of righteousness shall reign in life by one, (Jesus Christ.) Romans 5:17

And the Lord said, "If ye had faith as a grain of mustard seed, ye might say unto this sycamine tree, "Be thou plucked up by the root, and be thou planted in the sea; and it should obey you. Luke 17:6

My son, attend to my Words; incline thine ear unto my sayings.

Let them not depart from thine eyes; keep them in the midst of thine heart; For they are life unto those that find them, and health to all their flesh. Keep thy heart with all diligence; for out of it are the issues of life. Proverbs 4:20-23

So shall my Word be that goeth forth out of my mouth: it shall not return unto me void, but it shall accomplish that which I please, and it shall prosper in the thing whereto I sent it. Isaiah 55:11

2 For in many things we offend all. If any man offend not in Word, the same [is] a perfect man, [and] able also to bridle the whole body.

3 Behold, we put bits in the horse's mouths that they may obey us; and we turn about their whole body.

4 Behold also the ships, which though [they be] so great, and [are] driven of fierce winds, yet are they turned about with a very small helm, whithersoever the governor listeth.

5 Even so the tongue is a little member, and boasteth great things. Behold, how great a matter a little fire kindleth! James 3:2-5

Neither yield ye your members as instruments of unrighteousness unto sin: but yield yourselves unto God, as those that are alive from the dead, and your members as instruments of righteousness unto God. For sin shall not have dominion over you: for ye are not under the law, but under grace. Rom 6:13, 14

But if the Spirit of Him that raised up Jesus from the dead dwell in you, He that raised up Christ from the dead shall also quicken your mortal bodies by His Spirit that dwelleth in you. Roman 8:11

And Jesus knew their thoughts, and said unto them, "Every Kingdom divided against itself is brought to desolation; and every city or house divided against itself shall not stand: He that is not with me is against me; and he that gathereth not with me scattereth abroad. Matthew 12:25, 30

Pleasant Words are as a honeycomb, sweet to the soul, and health to the bones. Proverbs 16:24

A merry heart doeth good like a medicine: but a broken spirit drieth the bones. Proverbs 17:22

There is that speaketh like the piercings of a sword: but the tongue of the wise is health. Proverbs 12:18

Submit yourselves therefore to God. Resist the devil, and he will flee from you. James 4:7

I shall not die, but live, and declare the works of the LORD. Psalms 118:17

Bless the LORD, O my soul, and forget not all His benefits: Who satisfieth thy mouth with good things; so that thy youth is renewed like the eagle's. Psalms 103:2, 5

And ye shall serve the LORD your God, and He shall bless thy bread, and thy water; and I will take sickness away from the midst of thee. There shall be nothing to cast their young, nor be barren, in thy land: the number of thy days I will fulfill. Exodus 23:25, 26

Beloved, leave a good taste in your mouth and slap away every bad taste.

YHVH richly blesses you as you read this book, meditate, pray and make confessions of the scriptures.

Blessed be the Lord, who daily loadeth us with benefits, even the God of our salvation. Selah. Psalms 68:19

Enjoy His Benefits!!!

"The Greater One lives in me and He is bigger than any mountain, storm, power or situation I can ever face. My Father is greater than all and in the face of contrary circumstances; I declare YHVH lives big in me, and shows Himself mighty, on my behalf."

Please send your testimonies to sorministries@gmail.com

- Other books by the writer:
  - There Shall be A Performance
  - Let It Rain

Coming soon!!!

- Let It Rain 2
- The Sniper's Prayer
- The Power Of Sacrifice
- YHVH's Road Map

You may wish to write or call

sorministries@gmail.com

feovi@me.com

Address:

Sun of Righteousness Inc

P O. Box 72347

Phoenix Arizona 85050

Tel: 1-602-787-1508

www.sorministries.org

www.ingramcontent.com/pod-product-compliance
Lightning Source LLC
Chambersburg PA
CBHW071456070526
44578CB00001B/361